Plastic Practice

By

Chuck Noranel

1663 LIBERTY DRIVE, SUITE 200
BLOOMINGTON, INDIANA 47403
(800) 839-8640
WWW.AUTHORHOUSE.COM

First published by AuthorHouse 06/08/05

ISBN: 1-4208-2856-8 (sc)

Library of Congress Control Number: 2005902066

Printed in the United States of America
Bloomington, Indiana

This book is printed on acid-free paper.

<u>Acknowledgements</u>

Writing this story was the fulfillment of a dream. I was inspired by the limitless vision of several of my heroes, including Ronald Reagan, Pete Fountain, and Tom Wolfe. The joy and impact they have created from practicing and sharing their unique gifts inspired me to make this book my masterpiece.

I am indebted to many people for the feedback and suggestions that transformed this story into a finished novel. I particularly would like to thank:

Dr. Stephen DiJulio, for your very astute feedback and transformational insights.

Michael Flynn, for your friendship and lawsuit-preventing suggestions.

JoAnna Ventresca, for your encouragement to make this a full story.

My mother, for telling me the story is good, even though that's what mothers are supposed to do.

My son Harry, for being my best friend and providing ongoing encouragement.

My daughter Molly, for being a sweetheart and a source of joy.

Nelly Furtado and Norah Jones, two of the coolest, most beautiful, talented ladies in the world, who have given me hours of happiness and inspiration through their music. And for being the inspiration of my name, Nora…Nel.

First Galaxy Bank

Senior Executive Ranks & Not Senior Executive Ranks

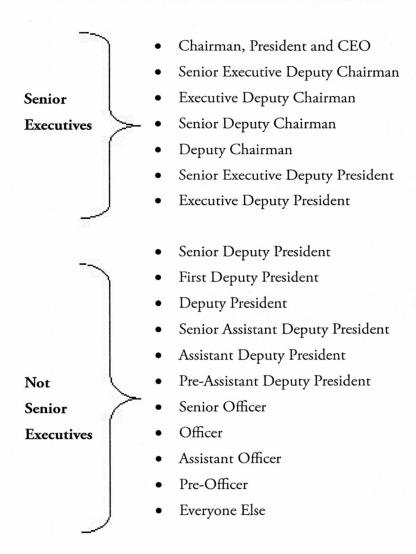

Senior Executives

- Chairman, President and CEO
- Senior Executive Deputy Chairman
- Executive Deputy Chairman
- Senior Deputy Chairman
- Deputy Chairman
- Senior Executive Deputy President
- Executive Deputy President

Not Senior Executives

- Senior Deputy President
- First Deputy President
- Deputy President
- Senior Assistant Deputy President
- Assistant Deputy President
- Pre-Assistant Deputy President
- Senior Officer
- Officer
- Assistant Officer
- Pre-Officer
- Everyone Else

Chapter One – Metal and Plastic

"Ouch!! Son of a motherless worthless sack of…"

"What did you say, dear? You want a sack of sunflower seeds?" Michelle Moore could hardly hear herself think over the piercing, grinding sound coming from the basement. Her husband Alan had been busy in his workshop all morning, bombarding the house with cussing, screaming and a bzzzzzzzzzzzzzzzzzzzzzzzz noise that sounded like a flock of parakeets flying into a buzz saw.

"What!! NO! I just cut myself with these ffu" Alan caught himself. His wife did not like cursing in the house, or anywhere else for that matter. "I cut myself with these dam… darn clippers. A metal shaving stayed on the ffffrigging blade and it hurts like a mother…. it hurts a lot." Bzzzzzzzzzzzzzzzzzzzzzzzz. Bzzzzzzzzzzzzzzzz.

Michelle couldn't take the noise any more and went down to the basement to talk with Alan. When she saw Alan, Michelle didn't know whether to laugh or feel pity. His face was dripping with sweat and covered with shiny metal specks that made him look like a rock musician after a glitter ball eruption. His tee shirt was soaked with sweat and streaked with grease and metal shavings. Hair dishevelment would have been at Carrot Top levels except that all the grease and sweat in his hair provided an unintended styling gel effect. Alan held a metal polisher in one bloody hand and was adjusting his dust covered eye goggles with his other hand.

"All right, Alan. What are you up to? I thought you had finished your clippers."

"I'm almost done. I've got to get the blades polished and smoothed before I run out of fingers and blood. I'm sorry for all the noise and screaming, but we've got a lot riding on" Alan was interrupted by the phone ringing upstairs. Sensing Michelle's irritation, he took advantage of the exit opportunity and ran upstairs to get it.

"Hello!"

"Hello. May I speak with Alan Moore please?" The caller ID said *"First Galaxy Bank."*

Alan felt the veins protrude from his forehead. He didn't need any more safe deposit boxes, car loans, equity loans, debit cards, coin wrappers, free calendars or anything else. What he needed…. wanted… was to not get any more calls from banks! His blood pressure was at Mt. St. Helens levels. The sweat running down his face was making his eyes sting. He could feel his face turning deepening shades of red.

"What is it? I'm in the middle of something!"

"Hello Mr. Moore. This is Mark Ruttle with First Galaxy. How are you today?"

"I just shit in my pants and I'm about to have a stroke. Enough small talk! **Get to the point!**"

"Mr. Moore, I'm calling about your First Galaxy Uranium Credit Card. I see that you have not made a payment since March, about 2 months ago."

"Well… you tracked me down Colombo! Congratulations on your ability to dial a phone! What are you going to do—send Rocco and Vito out to slap me around?" Alan was pissed.

"No sir. We're using Ivan and Mishka. The Russians are on the leading edge of collection techniques these days. Just kidding, Mr.

Moore. I'm an Account Manager in First Galaxy's Special Situations area. I'd like to discuss your situation and develop a plan to bring your account current."

"Yeah, right. If I want my legs broken, I'll borrow money from Silvio." A pretty reasonable response, Alan thought. The best defense is a good offense. Or is the best offense a good defense? Who gives a shit. This prick isn't going to push me around! He's probably some skinny geek with a paisley bow-tie who's too weak to push down a chair in a movie theater. Thinks he's a big man hiding behind his telephone. Let's see him do some real work instead of sitting in a chair blowing holes in his pants.

"Well sir, you've been a Customer for 3 years and until recently you managed the account superbly. We'd like to keep you as a Customer and see if we can work through your situation."

"Oh," was Alan's brilliant retort as the constructive statement from The Banker took some steam out of his engine. *Why won't this guy argue with me? Doesn't he know anything about Collections? Is he too important to argue?*

"Have you had any changes in your financial situation recently, Mr. Moore?"

"Uh, yeah. I just lost my job at Gibraltar Metal Products. I was there six years and was Senior Product Designer. The thing is, the only "metal product" they make is paper clips. With the shift to a paperless economy, the market for paper clips isn't what it used to be. Plus, the paper clip hasn't changed much in about 150 years, so my job was about as relevant as a moon-roof on a sailboat."

"I'm very sorry to hear that, Mr. Moore. What are your plans for now?"

"Well, they've given me 6 months severance, 1 month for every year I was there. My boss said if I can come up with a design for a new metal product, he might be able to restore my job."

"That sounds promising. How do you think it will work out?"

"Actually, and you're the first person besides my wife to hear this, I have an idea for a new metal product: *Dead Skin Clippers*. We have fingernail and toenail clippers, but nothing for dead skin. How much time do people spend every day peeling hardened, calloused skin from around their fingernails? A lot! If you don't do it right, it can hurt and cause bleeding. And I don't need to tell you the health consequences of open bleeding in today's society. This is a potential public health crisis and nothing is being done about it! Until now.

"*Dead Skin Clippers* look a lot like fingernail clippers, but instead of a concave curve, they have a slightly convex curve to grab the dead skin and leave the live skin in tact. In addition to selling them in drug, convenience and grocery stores, I want to put them in restaurants, bookstores and other places so people can clip dead skin whenever the need arises. They'd make a great option for cars as well, especially for people who commute in heavy traffic. I was putting the finishing touches on my prototype when you called. That's probably why I might have sounded a little angry before." Alan grabbed a pile of napkins to wipe his face. *Shit! Can't they make a friggin napkin that doesn't fall apart when you wipe the sweat off your face! Now I look like some idiot on his first day of shaving.*

4

"Man, that is a great idea," said Mark. "I can't tell you how many times I've been in a meeting or in the middle of a phone call and was distracted by pulling at some dead skin and I had nothing to use to clip it off. I'm going to buy the first one, Mr. Moore! It's good to hear about your proposal and the severance. Are you able to adjust any of your expenses while you finalize the proposal?"

"Yes. I've thought about it and I'm going to reduce some of the ongoing monthly stuff. I've already changed my Satellite TV package from *Double Platinum Premier* to *High-Gloss Bronze.* I told the trash company to downgrade me from *Platinum Pickup Concierge* to *Curbside Assistant.* And tomorrow I'm calling the cell phone company and changing from *Global Titanium Yap 24/7* to *Regional Brief-Talk.* These changes will save me about $200 a month. I'd like to keep my *Diamond Level Wireless Internet Service* for now, but I can save an additional $50 a month if I downscale to *Postal-speed Info Crawl.*"

"This is very helpful Mr. Moore. I appreciate you taking the time to provide this information. Now let's talk about a plan to bring your account current. Is that OK?"

"Yes," said Alan.

"Thank you. The total amount past due is $700 and your outstanding balance is $10,425. A payment of $400 by next Wednesday will keep your account from moving further past due. Additionally, once you make that $400 payment, there are several options we can offer you."

"That would be great," Alan responded. "I'll schedule the payment on your web site tonight, for next Wednesday. I've got to tell you, of all the creditors that have called, you're the only one to show some courtesy. You're really making an effort to help me through some difficult times and I appreciate it."

"That's our pleasure Mr. Moore. It's one of the key qualities that separates First Galaxy from other banks," answered Mark. "I'll talk with my Manager and get back to you tomorrow. Thank you for your time."

Alan was dumbfounded by the call. Was this bank really different? He figured he'd find out when Ruttle called back. If First Galaxy was on the level, he'd make every effort to pay them before any of the other banks that kept calling. Alan went downstairs to tell Michelle the news.

"Hey babe. Sorry for all the yelling. That was First Galaxy Bank. They're going to cut us some slack until I get my job back. I told the guy about my *Dead Skin Clippers* and he was real excited.

It looks like you got some metal dust on you. I better give you a thorough exam and get it all off you." After ten years of marriage, Alan still could not believe how lucky he was to have a beautiful wife like Michelle. Her silky black hair, radiant smile and warm voice made his heart jump. To make sure he got all the dust off, Alan started softly massaging Michelle's neck, back, shoulders, and.....

Who would have thought that a call from a bank would be an aphrodisiac?

Chapter 2 – Shunk 'N Jive

"Good moorrnnning! How ARE you?

"Good moorrnnning! How ARE you?

"Good moorrnnning! How ARE you?

"Good moorrnnning! How ARE you?"

Another day starts for Riichard Shunk, Executive Deputy President at First Galaxy Bank. Tall, thin and much younger looking than his 49 years, Riichard loved walking the hallways, greeting the underlings as he made his way to the cafeteria to get his morning tea. He was wearing his favorite brown plaid poly-fiber J'Bancs suit today, putting some extra bounce in his outlet-bought loafers.

As a **Senior Executive** at a **Major Financial Institution**, Riichard believed everyone loved him and was in awe of him. He actually believed most of the employees showed up to work each day to get one of his greetings. He gave everyone his most sincere-appearing greeting every morning:

> *Perfect posture, forward-leaning body language, head held high, brisk walking pace, big winning smile, topped off with a hearty* **"Good moorrnnning! How ARE you?"**

He had one of his secretaries keep count and his one-day greeting record was 38 "Good moorrnnnings!" That was the day the Building 3 Café was shut down, forcing everyone to walk to the cafe in Building 7 where Riichard had his office. Riichard thought they were there to get one of his "Good moorrnnnings!"

Riichard believed that "*Butts In Seats*," First Galaxy's daily measure of total attendance, had improved because of his greetings. In Riichard's mind, he could take credit for all achievements in the First Galaxy Headquarters Complex since employees showed up to see him. What leadership! What influence! What an impacting executive!

"Vikkie! Come in my office," Riichard announced to his secretary as he burst into his office suite upon returning from the café.

"Good morning Riich. What's up?"

"I am so excited. But first, look at these," Riichard said proudly.

Vikkie (everyone else called her Victoria, but Riichard used Vikkie because he liked to show how close he was to his staff) looked puzzled.

"These." Riichard squealed, showing off his newly monogrammed shirt cuffs. He had both cuffs and his shirt pocket monogrammed with a bold **"RAS."** *Now that's class*, thought Riichard.

"Oh, you got your shirt monogrammed," Vikkie noticed. "Is that one of the new shirts you got at Simm's Basement?"

"Yes, yes it is. What a great buy. The shirts were marked down to $19.95 from $129.95. I know because they had red cross-outs on the original price. They had just my size too: 15 ½ neck, 35" sleeves, fitted. My size hasn't changed since I was in high school. I wear fitted shirts because I am in exceptional shape because I exercise every morning."

"Wow! That is so cool," Vikkie squeaked. She had heard this story 1,000 times, but Riichard liked her to be adoring and supportive. "The purple in your shirt really brings out the plaid pattern in your suit.

And it's totally cool the way you matched up a striped shirt, striped tie and plaid suit. You really dress well Riich."

"That's a very important part of leadership, Vik. You know, I have over 25 suits. My size hasn't changed since I was in high school. The Master Tailors at J' Bancs love me. The last time I was there, they asked me if they could put my picture in the dressing rooms, to inspire their customers.

"Vik, I had the best idea just now. You know what a thrill everyone gets from my morning greetings? Well, that's just here at Global Headquarters. I was looking at the *Butts In Seats* stats for First Galaxy's other sites and they're lower than here. You know why that is?"

"I'm not sure Riich. You're so smart. What do you think?" Vikkie asked in the excited, encouraging tone Riich liked.

"Close the door and I'll tell you." Riich liked to have his door closed. He did not like interruptions. "That's a beautiful skirt. Is the material silk or is it gabardine?"

"It's polyester, silly. I can't afford silk."

Vikkie was 19 years old and had been at First Galaxy about 4 months. She filled the vacancy when Riich's previous secretary left suddenly for personal reasons. Riich told Vikkie that he and Steffie had been very close and were great friends. He hoped that he and Vikkie would be as close as he and Steffie. Vikkie applied for a job at First Galaxy after Riich visited her school as part of his High School Outreach program. Riich was very dedicated to recruiting young people. He took it as a personal mission to reach out to young people and develop them into great leaders like him. He devoted many hours to this important role.

"Stick with me and one day you will be able to afford silk, Vik. Anyway, back to my idea. The reason *Butts In Seats* is lower at the other First Galaxy sites is because I only have a presence here, at Global HQ. I want you to schedule me for visits to every First Galaxy site. I'll need to have rolling visits of 3 days each so I can establish a pattern of providing my morning greetings at each site. Once the employees at the other sites start to expect my greetings, *Butts In Seats* will grow.

"Each visit should be Thursday, Friday and Monday. That means we'll need to stay over on the weekends and I will really miss my family, but as a Senior Executive I must make the sacrifice. We'll need to leave by mid-day on Wednesdays to ensure we're fresh and ready for Thursday morning. Returns will be Tuesday mid-morning, so I can do my greetings on Tuesday mornings before returning to Global HQ. That will give us a few hours in the office prior to returning to the field. Let's see, that makes um… 4 morning greetings and …… 6 overnights for each site visit. I can picture *Butts In Seats* growing already!

"Schedule a meeting for me with Joel Stanton in Internet Initiatives. Provide him a schedule of my trips so he can post them on the First Galaxy Daily Intranet Site. Make sure he just posts the schedule on the part of the site that the low level employees see. There's no need to have my peers in the executive suite know about this. You know how jealous they can be even though they're all my friends. I'll give them an update once *Butts In Seats* gets bigger.

"All this talk about butts reminds me: You'll be going with me on these trips. This will be an important part of your leadership training and give you a chance to see how a Senior Executive operates. I'll put together an agenda for the trips and you can fill in the details. Book all the travel and hotel stuff on your company credit card. That way I can approve the expenses and won't waste my bosses' time signing expense reports. OK." [big exaggerated swoop of his arm to look at his watch] "I've got to run to an important meeting out of the bank. I'll be back later. Page me if you need me. Thaannnkkssssss."

By the time the hiss of the "thaannnkkssss" was finished, Riich was out the door.

Chapter 3 – Interest In Common Sense

"DAMN IT!! WHAT KIND OF PILE OF SHIT IS THIS?!"

The Chairman slammed the phone down so hard it caused the Faberge egg across the room to rattle in its 24-karat gold perch.

Harold "Rolly" Burnrock, Chairman, CEO and President of First Galaxy Bank was disappointed. One of his assistants just phoned with some bad news: His Maybach Custom Edition Model 62 with serial number 001 would not be ready for two more days. Rolly had to have it TOMORROW! He had waited for 18 months to get this car. He had personally placed the order with Franz Gundhieghter, Daimler-Chrysler CEO and HAD TO be the first person in the U.S. to take delivery. There was a Major Fundraising Event at The Burnrock Estate tomorrow evening and Rolly wanted the Maybach on display out front where all his guests would see it. A new platinum-edged platform had been installed at The Estate for the car, but now there would be no car!

"Ted! This is what happens when you put junior level employees in charge of important things. What level is my dip-shit assistant, Pastere?" Rolly asked his Senior Executive Deputy Chairman, Ted Reilly. Ted was in his 21st year with Rolly and was accustomed to his rants. Ted had an almost pastoral level of patience and calm, making him a good counter-point to Rolly's volatile manner.

"Brad Pastere is a First Deputy President, Rolly," Ted replied.

"No wonder he's as effective as a 1-inch dick in a sperm-donor factory. Make him Senior Deputy President and give him a $20,000 raise. Screw that. Make it Executive Deputy President, then he'll be part of the Senior Executive group. Even though he's about as useful as a case of Viagra in a eunuch's home, he represents Me and will be titled accordingly. How can an assistant to the CEO of the largest credit card bank in the world not be at least an Executive Deputy President? What the hell is wrong with you Ted? The kid's been busting his ass.

"**HELEN,** get that kraut bastard Franz Gundhieghter on the phone," Rolly yelled to his Secretary.

Rolly looked up and saw his Most Senior Executives sitting at the conference table in his office. "When did you get in here? Let's start the meeting."

It was 7:00 AM on the dot and time for the Morning Management Meeting. Rolly held one every day at 7:00 to ensure his executive team kept a sense of urgency and clarity about First Galaxy's strategic direction and core values. First Galaxy was the largest credit card bank in the U.S. Rolly was the founding Chairman of First Galaxy and very proud of its consistent performance and leading position among U.S. corporations. Rolly was an imposing figure, even though he was only 5'6" in height. He had thick black hair, parted on the right like Ronald Reagan. He had massive shoulders from childhood summers spent helping his father load and deliver cinderblocks. Rolly was an impeccable dresser, exclusively wearing custom-tailored Oxxford suits, Super 150s fabric or better. Rolly's deep, resonant voice was the epitome of CEO. A cigar aficionado, Rolly was rarely seen without a Don Carlos Presidente in hand. Some joked that the size of the cigar made up for inadequacies in other areas, but they were careful to do so well outside the hearing range of the Chairman.

Rolly looked at the three executives around the table with pride. He brought each of them to First Galaxy over 20 years ago and developed the leadership potential he had seen in them. Rolly was a genius in many respects, including his ability to assemble and nurture a core management team at First Galaxy. He was proud of his executive team.

None of the executives, including Rolly, came from wealth. All had worked their way through college. They were all motivated to grow and protect the precious jewel that was First Galaxy. Rolly created a culture of treating the employees of First Galaxy with respect and believed that a major challenge in the years ahead would be to maintain First Galaxy's strong core values as the company became larger and less personable.

First Galaxy employees were paid the highest salaries in the industry and had a variety of incentive programs to reward achievement of company goals. The company provided best-in-class health care benefits, in-house tanning salons, free cell phones, 1-hour photo processing, postal services, restaurant-quality cafeterias, free MP3 downloads from the company intranet site, on-site oil changes and car wash, free office delivery of the local newspaper and more.

Rolly loved to tell the story of how First Galaxy had come to Delaware. The story began in the late 1970's, when Jimmy Carter's economic policies were in full bloom: Double-digit inflation, high unemployment, shortages of key energy supplies and raw materials, increasing government regulation and record high interest rates. Economic policies were focused on managing scarcity and allocating pain, not on growth and opportunity. These conditions were bad for all businesses, particularly banks.

Since a bank's inventory is money, high inflation and high interest rates devalue the inventory and make it difficult to issue loans. What was the point of loaning $1.00, only to be paid back with inflation-ravaged dollars worth $0.80?

The situation was particularly egregious for credit card banks. Social engineering by state legislatures had created usury laws that capped the interest rate banks could assess on credit cards. Of course, there was no cap on what it *cost* banks to raise money (nor should there have been). As with many policies created by politicians, it hurt the people it was designed to help.

With interest rates in the high teens, it cost credit card banks more to raise money than they could charge to lend money. Pay 18% for money and loan it out for 12% and you won't be in business very long. With the laws of supply and demand in a straight-jacket, lending dried up. Consumers could not borrow; businesses could not borrow; the economy was starved of its fundamental source of growth: money.

When a large vacuum is created, the power of the free market will fill the void. Two states, Delaware and South Dakota, had the courage and vision to create real-world economic policies and eliminated their usury laws. The vacuum quickly filled as virtually every credit card bank in the U.S. relocated operations to one of these two states, enabling a key element of the U.S. economic growth engine, consumer activity, to re-start.

Did interest rates on credit cards soar as a result? Were people making weekly trips to the bank to pay the "vig" on their credit card loans? Did Banks use lack of usury laws to gouge Customers? No. Market forces of supply and demand kept rates at appropriate levels. Since the mid-1990's, credit card interest rates became increasingly competitive. Thus, two states played a key role in enabling the U.S. economic engine to run full speed ahead.

This is what led First Galaxy to move its operations to Delaware from Massachusetts. In Delaware, First Galaxy found a business-friendly state with excellent living conditions, a large, well-educated populace and a strategic location near Washington, New York and Philadelphia. Within a few years, Rolly and First Galaxy went from being one of a cast of thousands in Massachusetts to one of the largest players on the Delaware economic, political and social scene.

"Loans," Rolly focused on each of the key business drivers every day.

"Loans were up $200 million yesterday. Strong retail activity related to the start of the summer vacation season was a key driver. We are on track to hit Plan for month end," reported Tom Hughman, Senior Executive Deputy Chairman, responsible for the operations side of First Galaxy. Tom Hughman and Ted Reilly were peers and the top two executives below Rolly.

Tom had been with Rolly for most of the last 19 years, except for an 18 month period devoted to competitive mountain climbing. This earned Tom the nickname 'Alps' upon his return to First Galaxy. Where Ted was a natural calm, Tom was more of a forced calm. He had a no-nonsense, skip-the-b.s. style and generally tolerated Rolly's idiosyncrasies, but occasionally snapped back. Tom was 5'4" and the shortest of the executive team, so Rolly sometimes called him 'Mini-Alps.'

"How certain are you that Plan will be achieved?" Rolly asked. The Plan was the roadmap First Galaxy followed to maintain its growth and leadership position in the industry. Rolly was relentless in pushing his team to achieve and exceed The Plan. Part of Rolly's genius was his ability to set very aggressive goals and have the staff and infrastructure in place to achieve them.

"Yesterday's loans were $30 million above month-end target. With four business days remaining in the month, we're confident of achieving Plan. The Call Centers are ready with special offers if loans slip," answered Ted Reilly, responsible for First Galaxy's marketing activities. He wanted Rolly to know they had contingency plans in place to hit the Plan. Ted was 5'5" and very thin. His nickname was 'Reed.' "We're $30 million ahead of Plan?" Rolly asked.

"Yes, and we…," Ted started.

"Increase the Plan by $40 million. I want to keep the $30 million and add $10 million more. If the market's as strong as you're indicating, get more market share now." Rolly directed.

"Accounts," Rolly moved on to the next key driver.

"Delinquency." "Call Volume." "Call Time." The updates continued. Adjustments were made as Rolly deemed necessary.

"*Butts In Seats*. What is going on here? The trend is down in all sites except Global Headquarters," Rolly asked.

"Well Rolly, we're looking into it," replied Breeze Penner. Breeze, a Senior Executive Deputy President, was responsible for all the administrative areas of First Galaxy. Breeze was the son of Rolly's wife's brother. Many people called Breeze "LQ" in honor of his low IQ. Breeze was so dumb that he didn't even know it was an insult. He thought a low IQ, like low cholesterol and low weight, was a good thing. Breeze was 5'9" tall, an attribute that was sufficient to earn Rolly's taunts. LQ's ignorance was at such a Mensa-like level that he thought the stream of insults flowing in his direction were compliments. "We've commissioned an internal staff satisfaction survey and are thinking about conducting special training sessions with all department managers to address the situation. I'll get back to you soon about the plans to fix *Chairs In Seats*, Rolly."

"I'll bet you came up with those ideas all by yourself, LQ. I know you have the attention span of a bubble, but we're talking about *Butts In Seats*, not *Chairs In Seats*. Get me an answer tomorrow morning. This is unacceptable," Rolly said.

Damn, Breeze thought. *I knew I had a great attention span, but I didn't know that Rolly knew it too! I like bubbles.*

"Tom, what is this memo I got from Wallace Malvagio?" Rolly asked.

"Not sure," said Tom. "May I see it?" Tom quickly scanned the memo from Malvagio, the Chief Financial Officer, who had been with First Galaxy for 3 years. Wallace Malvagio came to First Galaxy after a 20 year career with numerous New York money center banks. Wallace thought First Galaxy was an old fashioned, fat, benevolent company that stumbled along to success. He viewed it as his mission to make First Galaxy lean and mean, with emphasis on the *mean*, a trait he learned and enjoyed in New York. Wallace had a bank vault tattooed on his left fore arm and a dollar sign on his right fore arm as a sign of his devotion to banking. He didn't consider credit cards to be 'real' banking like they did on The Street, but when his last bank pushed him out following a merger, he figured he would teach the backwoods hacks in Delaware how to run a business. Wallace was known as 'Class', because he folded his suit jacket open to show the Armani label he had sewn inside and because he wore his Tag Heuer 8-dial Chronograph pushed halfway up his hand.

"It must be in transit to me, Rolly. I have not seen it yet. I'll talk to Class about it," Tom replied. Wallace was again recommending a staff reduction of 25%, primarily from layoffs. He sent these memos to Rolly a few times each year. Class hated people and loved numbers. He believed his numbers would not look right until there were far fewer employees at First Galaxy.

"Meeting over. HELEN, where is Franz Gundhieghter?"

"It's late afternoon in Germany. He's giving the German Chancellor a tour of a new manufacturing plant and will be tied up for another 30 minutes," Helen Sullivan replied through the intercom. Helen had been Rolly's Executive Assistant for over 12 years.

"**Get him on the phone NOW**. I'll dump every Mercedes First Galaxy owns and never buy another one."

"One moment, sir. There is a Mr. Heinz Dreighten, President of the Maybach Division on the line who is ready to assist you," Helen offered.

"Put him on!" "**HELLO?** Dreighten? What kind of shit operation are you running? I've seen better service from a Yugo dealership. Where is my "62"? If you were half as fast delivering the car as you bastards were taking my money I could have driven to the moon by now."

"Jahvohl, Mr. Burnrock. It is a pleasure to speak with you. I am sorry for the inconvenience we have caused you. If you will allow, I can explain the reason for the delay," said Dreighten.

"Go ahead, I don't have all damn day."

"The car is completely finished and inspected from a mechanical and interior perspective. The craftsmanship is wonderful! There has been a one day delay in receiving the diamonds you ordered for the rear seat DVD controls. We also installed a radio custom programmed to only play music from the 1940's and 1950's, as you requested. So, other than the diamonds, the car is completely ready. I understand that time is critical, so I would propose we deliver the car to you this evening and follow up to install the diamonds later this week, with all apologies for the inconvenience we have caused. We would like to offer you an upgraded headlamp heating system as way of apology. Would this be acceptable to you, Mr. Burnrock?"

"My assistant, Mr. Pastere, will contact you to make the arrangements. Make sure you congratulate him. He was just promoted." Rolly slammed down the phone, further loosening the Faberge egg from its perch.

At the Maybach offices in Bonn, the staff could hear the usually mild-mannered Franz Dreighten yelling. "MEIN SCHLECHTES SCHÖNES MAYBACH, STARK GEHEND ZU WIE SCHLAG! SIE SOLLTEN IHN ZU DEN VORDEREN LINIEN IM IRAK GESCHICKT HABEN!" [My poor Maybach, going to such a moron! They should have sent him to the front lines in Iraq!] One thing Franz did like about America was the bourbon. He kept a bottle in his desk for use after interactions with Rolly and other executives who believed the axis of the earth rotated around their greatness. Rolly was about the worst he dealt with. The only executive who was more of a prima-donna was a real estate executive in New York who ordered car seats molded to fit the shape of his ass. There was also the Hollywood director, who traveled to his important environmental and homeless events in an 8-ton armored Mercedes limo. The director insisted that every car door played a song from one of his movies when opened or closed. Franz took a long pull from the bottle and placed a call to Maybach of Delaware to make sure the delivery went perfectly. He also made a note to insert a $7,000 charge for the 'upgraded headlamp system.' Franz told Rolly they would offer it to him; he didn't say anything about not charging for it.

Chapter 4 – Mr. 35

"Ohmigod and then you know what the dork did after that?" Vikkie was on the phone with one of her friends. She had lots of free time at work since Riich was rarely in the office.

"What did he do? Take it out and put it on your desk?" Vikkie's friend Barb giggled.

"No you perv. Besides, I don't have a microscope so how would I see it? He had me close the door to his office so he could look at my butt. Then the schmuck said (high-pitched voice) 'oh, is that silk?' when he saw my skirt. He makes me want to puke all over his parted-down-the-middle hair. Then he shines me with how I'll be dressing in silk if I stick with him. I'd rather be the free attraction at *Whore Night at the Senior Center* than even touch him. He was wearing this hideous brown suit with a plaid pattern and he had a striped shirt and striped tie. He looked like a TV test pattern during a thunderstorm. I told him how good it looked and he lapped it up. Oh, and now he's come up with some boondoggle idea about visiting every First Galaxy site in the country and he wants me to tag along. I think he thinks I'll want to sit in daddy's lap on the airplane."

"Why do you put up with his shit, Vik?" Barb asked.

"I get paid $32 a year to do nothing, that's why. He's never actually *done* anything, he just insinuates all the time. Plus, he ditches most of the time so I hardly even see him. Wait… that's him calling now! Hold on!"

"First Galaxy Bank, Riichard Shunk's office, this is Victoria."

"Hellloo." Riich gave his trademark cheerful greeting. He pronounced "hello" like a three-syllable word. "Hey Vikk! How's everything? [*evvvrreeethingg*] I'm just about to pull into the garage. What's up?"

"Your wife called several times. I told her you were in back-to-back meetings like you are every day because you're on many important committees, just like you told me to tell her. She said something about a meeting with a counselor at Privilege Preparatory Academy."

"Yeah yeah yeah I know about that. It's, um it's, the counselor wants to meet with me to talk about moving Anna into the gifted program. The counselor there loves me and is always asking me to join the um Academic Advisory Board. Gotta go. I'm pulling into the gar...." The line cut out.

"Barb, I've gotta go. Dickless is pulling into the garage."

One hour later, Riich burst into his suite, fast paced, forward-leaning, the image of a Very Important Executive. Even though it was 4:30 in the afternoon, his appearance was fresh and pressed, his energy level higher than when the day started. Victoria used to wonder where Riich's energy level came from, but became used to it when she noticed many other First Galaxy execs with the same level of vibrancy and aliveness.

"Hey there, Vik. Any messages," Riich asked, breezing into his office.

"Just your wife. And a James Quill called. Wouldn't leave a number. Said you would know what it was about."

"Yeah yeah yeah. James is one of my best friends. He's a great friend of mine. Hey Vik, in between meetings today, I sketched out the agenda for my *Butts In Seats* visits. How about if you take the lead and fill in the details and stuff. Where did the day go? I'm in so many important meetings and so many people need to talk with me that the days just fly by. Gotta go. Any plans for tonight? See you tomorrow." Riich handed Victoria the agenda and was out the door, 4:40 on the dot.

**Butts In Seats – Riichard Shunk Executive Visit
Daily Agenda**

- 1 hour - Exercise in hotel fitness center (note: have memberships arranged in advance)
- 25 minutes - Shower
- 30 minutes - Breakfast – day planning
- 30 minutes – Greetings for Butts In Seats
- Return to Hotel
- 1 hour – Lunch
- Return to Hotel
- 1 hour - High School Outreach
- Return to Hotel
- 30 minutes – Drinks, hotel bar – Dinner planning
- 2 hours - Dinner with High School Outreach student guests
- -- Drinks, hotel bar – Dinner and day review; next day planning

Notes to Vik: 1. You will be involved in all of these except High School Outreach. 2. Make hotel reservations where I have points programs and make sure your room and my room are booked under my program number. 3. Rent a Cadillac Escalade in white or gold. 4. Thanks Vik!!! from Riich☺

Richard Antoine Shunk was born 49 years earlier in Purchase, New York. As the years progressed, "Purchase" was dropped and it became "New York" to give the impression he was from Manhattan.

Riich received an associate certificate from East Albany State Community College. Riich quickly tired of hearing *"East Albany State? Where is that?"* so to help people more easily understand his background, he simply said he went to State University of New York. Upon receiving his certificate degree, he worked in marketing and sales positions for various cosmetics companies.

Riich's big break came in 1990 when his parents took a vacation to Scotland. While on a tour of the Johnny Walker Distillery in Kilmarnock, his parents met a lovely American couple, Rolly and Katie Burnrock. The two couples hit it off while sampling the distillery's products. Stan Shunk was a partner in the oldest law firm in Purchase and was familiar with many of the regulatory issues facing banks. This impressed Rolly greatly as did Stan's love of antique horse shoes. When the subject turned to family, Rolly learned the Shunk's had a son, Richard. Stan and Mabel Shunk were privately concerned that their son worked at a ladies cosmetics company and used some gentle spin to create some interest from Rolly.

"Have him give me a call." Rolly said after listening to the Shunks' glowing description of their version of Richard's credentials. We always need good executive talent and strong leaders. Based on your description of Richard's academic excellence, college athletic achievements and position as Marketing Director at the local bank, he'll be an asset to First Galaxy," said Rolly.

Riich was hired as a First Deputy President shortly after Rolly returned from vacation. He was hired after receiving a call from one of the Chairman's assistants. *Hired without an interview! Wow, I really am top notch.*

Riich loved the fast-paced environment at First Galaxy. Coming in as a hire recommended by the Chairman, he rode an assured path to success. Within two years, Riich had been promoted twice, achieving the level of Executive Deputy President. He loved the word "reach." It reminded him of himself. He also knew that Rolly loved enthusiastic, positive achievers. That gave him an idea: *Add another "i" to my name.* Thus, "Rich" became "Riich," pronounced as "reach." What better way to demonstrate commitment than changing his name to help the company succeed?

Riich was primarily known as "Dick Boy," "Shithead," and "Mr. 35" by people who knew him at First Galaxy. Riich loved to tell everyone that "I've had 35 jobs here at First Galaxy!" To him, it was a sign of experience, involvement and being in demand. To others, it showed he had the impact of a sprig of parsley: purely there for show, providing nothing of substance. He went into each new "opportunity" with his own image front of mind, fully expecting to be moved to another area as soon as he left his magic touch. He would move on believing that a new group of "best friends" had been created who "were very sorry to see me go and said I was the best manager they ever had."

Every Thursday at 5:00, Riich held a staff meeting. He made sure Vik booked the conference room with the big glass windows on the 2nd floor by the main elevators. That way, the employees that walked by on their way out would see Riich and his group hard at work after hours.

He also knew that the Chairman sometimes walked past this particular conference room and welcomed the opportunity to be seen spending time with his staff.

Riich opened each meeting with an update on his current activities, so the staff could benefit from hearing how a Senior Executive of a Major Financial Institution spent his time.

"Heyyy my friends. Thannnkksss for coming. How's evvvreeethinngggg? I hope I'm not keeping you from anything because you know how important it is to balance work and family. You would not believe how many times my daughter has been in tears because I got home late since I stay late at work everyday because there is just so much to do and I am in so many important meetings. If any of you need guidance on getting the proper balance, get on my calendar with Vik and she'll try to squeeze you in. Um, Vikkie, I'm down to my last box of red felt-tip pens. I need you to get me some more please. I've been in a lot of Important Meetings lately. I met with Rolly two days ago about the 2005 Plan. It went great. Everything is looking great. Last night, I had dinner with a bunch of football guys, um….. Paul Taglabow, Jimmy James and Al Mitchells. What a great bunch of guys they are." Riich could sense how impressed everyone was. He could tell because there was total silence. He held their rapt attention. *"This is touching," Riich thought. "Look how in awe of me they are. They're hanging on my every word. I really do make the little people feel better."*

"What a lying sack of shit," Mort Grack thought. Mort was a Senior Deputy President in the Banker Market, the department that reported to Riich. Mort had seen something on the *Daily Digest* (First Galaxy's intranet site) about a video of a recent presentation Rolly gave to some

Wall Street Analysts. The video was shown to all Senior Executives two days ago when "Riich met with Rolly." Mort knew the 'dinner with the football guys' was a crock because there was a big charity fundraiser with League executives at the Riverfront Arts Center last night.

"OK, Mort how are you doing on accounts? Are you making me look good?"

"Riich, I've been trying to get with you. We're tracking well below goal because…." Out of the corner of his eye, Mort saw the Chairman leaving for the night.

Riich did a Big Exaggerated Swoop of his arm to look at his watch.

"Gotta run guys. I have an uh a important… Little Achievers Executive Board Meeting tonight. I think they're going to ask me to become Acting Chairman. See you tomorrow. Thannnkkksssss," Riich squealed as he left the group with the sssss still hanging in the air.

"Well guys. Since we're here, how about if we work on some ideas for getting our marketing on track?" Mort asked the group. The group agreed, because they wanted to do their best for First Galaxy.

So far this year, the Banker Market was the furthest behind goal for account production. Last year, Bankers was the 2nd highest account producer for First Galaxy. That was when Cindy Glodspeck lead the Market. Riich had upped the account goal when he joined the group after Cindy was moved to another area in February. He wanted to show he could do better than Cindy. Plus, he knew Rolly liked people who set aggressive goals. Unfortunately, Riich's whereabouts were not known when meetings were held to create the budget dollars for marketing the accounts. All the other Markets were represented at these vital meetings to allocate marketing resources. This left the Banker Market with an increased goal and no money to achieve it. Riich did not like to be bothered with these types of "details" and blamed the lack of funding on Mort, who as a Senior Deputy President did not participate in the resource allocation meetings, yet another "detail" too trivial to merit Riich's attention.

At 6:00, the Banker Market team was still at work when Ted Reilly, Senior Executive Deputy Chairman and Chief Marketing Officer walked past the conference room. *"Good, the Banking team is working late. Riich really has them pumped up and motivated. I'll send him a note of thanks for the great work he's doing,"* Ted thought.

Chapter 5 – Meetin' & Reportin'

"Amma amma amma goot goot goot. Let's am uh lash right into it. We'll get crackin and put a ringed fence around it!" Barney O'Farkle, Senior Executive Deputy President and Director of Special Situations, said as way of greeting Mark Ruttle and his manager, Liddy Yeest.

Barney had moved to the United States 11 years earlier. Originally from Ireland, his accent was as thick as the day he left the mother country.

Barney's ticket to First Galaxy was stamped the day he married Trina Stream, a First Galaxy manager who was in the Chairman's favor. A spouse of someone the Chairman liked was definite executive material. Husband and wife were both promoted to Senior Executive Deputy President shortly after their marriage, the first time promotions had been given as a wedding present.

Mark and Liddy had developed a plan for bringing Alan Moore's account up to date and needed to get Barney's approval. They had asked for a meeting two days earlier due to the time sensitivity, but Barney had not been available. Month-end was approaching and they wanted to clear up as many delinquencies as possible.

"Barney, we'd like to update you on the Alan Moore account and ask your approv," Liddy began.

"What? Who was that again? Is that one of the lads amma tardy on amma one of his accounts? I saw it on one of me reports somewhere, yeah?" inquired Barney.

"Yes, Barney, Mr. Moore has a balance of $10,500, of which"

"JAYZUS! 10,500! Is that dollars or pounds? How do these people get themselves into such fixes?" Barney wondered. Barney had no difficulty paying *his* bills with a base salary of $525,000 + 125% bonus, and could not understand why other people did not manage their finances as well as he did. He was pretty sure that Trina made even more than he did, but they kept separate accounts.

"The balance is in dollars. About $400 is past due and the account will cycle in 2 days. To keep it from"

"What? Is it amma all payin them finance charges and what about ummmm late fees? Are we collectin all of that there on it?" Barney interjected.

"Yes, the full balance has been revolving due to its past due status. Mark had a good conversation with Mr"

"What? How much have we got from them umma late fees there? What was it the lad bought with the card anyway? We should look to see if we could re um, re re.... umma amma amma re-am what is it I wuz gonna say, umma position, yes re-position the stuff he bought if any of it has any value, ya know?"

"Yes, yes. We have an itemized list of the merchandise Mr. Moore purchased and if necessary will pursue re-possession. However, since credit card accounts are unsecured, we'd need to get Mr. Moore's approval. The good news is that Mark had a good conversation with Mr. Moore about his monthly exp"

"Goot goot goot. Do ya need me to give Mr. Moore a shout and amma amma go through this with him? Why don't you set up a meetin to call him. We'll need to have a pre-meetin to prepare for the actual meetin, ya know! I got me some reports here somewhere talking about this type of stuff. **SILLEEEEEE! What did you do with them am amma reports?**" Barney yelled out to his secretary, Sally.

Barney's office was spontaneous combustion in-waiting. Every available surface was buried with reports, old newspapers, magazines, empty food containers, cups and soda cans. The shelves of his credenza were so tightly packed with over-stuffed binders that a few weeks earlier the side panels of the credenza exploded from the outward pressure. The force of the flying notebooks and credenza pieces broke the glass walls in the front of Barney's office, sending glass flying everywhere. Several employees with cubicles near the front of his office were cut pretty seriously by the flying glass. Barney was very agitated by the explosion and interrupted a phone call to place his lunch order to deal with the situation. "Amma Ian I need to put a bookmark on me feed order for a minute. Some of me reports just left me office. Be a lad and hold on a few ticks." Barney walked out of his office and approached the nearest employee he saw, sitting in her cubicle. "Amma amma, Miss Clerk, I mean... [craning his neck to read her name plate] amma Miss Tomson, some of me reports went flyin your way. Did ya happen to retrieve any of the lads? When yer done whatever it is yer doin, could ya be a lass and fetch them for me. I'm busier than a one-armed juggler at the circus and I need them for some meetins, ya know!" Unfortunately, Miss Thomas was too busy getting broken glass off her clothes and wiping blood off her face to look for Barney's reports. Frustrated by the lack of concern for his reports, Barney returned to his office to finish his phone call. "Ian, my lad, I'm back. Give me the large corn beef sub with extra mayo and vinegar. Make it the double-large. Give me a triple order of chips and a medium diet. Put it on me business account and lay in a ½ pound tip for yourself, ya know! Tap." Barney scribbled a note to his secretary, Sally to give Maintenance a shout to get his windows fixed and his credenza repaired. He also told Sally to send out a memo to the floor staff reminding them to keep their cubicles sharp and shined. He was aghast at all the loose papers the underlings left lying about like an animals' cage.

Liddy tried to get Barney focused on the topic at hand. "We appreciate your offer to get involved, Barney. Mark has worked up a plan and we just need you to sign right here on this,"

"What? This form here? Amma right where the ummm ammm SIGN HERE stick thing is? OK, it's done and dusted. This will lower our delinquency by how much? I need to give amma amma amma me update to Tom Hughman at one of his meetins."

"It will bring this account current for now, but one account won't benefit the total delinq"

"What? I've got to run. I'm late for a meetin. I'm meetin with Purchasing ya know about me new desk blotter. It was ordered weeks ago and I'm finding out if it's on the bottom of the sea, ya know! And I need me leather chair reconditioned too."

"Well, we got what we wanted," said Liddy to Mark after Barney dashed out of the office.

"Yes. I'll call Mr. Moore and let him know we'll put him on a special payment plan to help him get current. It's nice to work at a company that helps people," said Mark.

"You did great work on this, Mark. You really put your interpersonal skills and creative analytical skills to work to maintain

Mr. Moore's loyalty. I'll be sure to let Barney, I mean, I'll be sure to note it on your review." said Liddy.

"Thank you Liddy. I'll call Mr. Moore soon as I get back to my desk."

What a load! Liddy thought. *I've got more knowledge in one of my fingernails than Barney has in his whole whale-sized body. How long can I play Charity Host for this loser? I like my job and helping our Customers, but I'm tired of going through this endless maze to get things done. I wonder if other large companies operate like this.*

"Hello, Mr. Moore? This is Mark Ruttle with First Galaxy."

"Hi, Mark. How's it going?" Alan answered.

"Great. How is the *Dead Skin Clipper* business?"

"Fantastic. I've already got a contract to sell them in Hair Clippery locations in the Northeast U.S. They're going to combine the *Dead Skin Clipper* with a new "nose hair buzz cut" service. Hair Clippery said if it's successful, they might expand into ear hair trimming as well. I'm really pumped.

"I talked to my boss at Gibraltar and he was so happy he promoted me to Executive Product Designer and gave me a raise. Plus, I'm going to get a 5% royalty on every *Dead Skin Clipper* sold. I even used an idea from you credit card banks and set up different quality levels of *Dead Skin Clipper*: Tin, Gold, Platinum, and Titanium. They all do exactly the same thing, but some cost more than others."

"Congratulations, Mr. Moore! I'm happy for you. Remember, I want one of the first ones. As a matter of fact, I've got a piece of dead skin hanging from my thumb right now. I was just in a very tedious meeting and occupied myself by pulling at some old hardened skin."

"I already put a set in the mail to you, Mark. As it turns out, I won't need to go into any of the special programs you have, but I greatly appreciate the way you worked with me when it looked like I was going to be facing some tough times. I should be able to make a $1,000 payment by the end of next week, which will get me ahead of the game."

"Thank you, Mr. Moore. I just received approval to offer you a special program, but I'm glad things have turned around for you. Please let us know if we can ever be of service to you in the future."

"Thanks, Mark. Good-bye."

Chapter 6 – Acting Professional

George Kreble loved his job. As Chairman of The Society of Certified Practitioners he led the largest professional organization in the world. The Society was a must-join organization of all practicing professionals, including doctors, dentists, lawyers, and educators. Over 6 million professionals paid $1,500 per year for the prestige of membership. In return, members received Practice Management Support (accounting, financial, technology), exclusive access to top resorts around the world, access to political leaders, and a powerful lobbying voice at the federal and state level.

George and his staff were comfortably located on the 72nd and 73rd floors of the Global Tower in Chicago. George had spectacular views of Chicago and Lake Michigan from his corner suite on the 73rd floor. A serious audiophile, George was glad his 600 square foot office was large enough for a full high-end audio set-up: Lexicon MC-12 Processor, Classe Omega Amps, Aerial 20T Speakers with custom mahogany finish, MIT Shotgun cables, custom electrical supply, and sonically optimized room treatments.

George invited his advisors from Overture Ultimate Audio to visit from Wilmington, Delaware twice a year to tweak the system and brief him on the latest advancements in the audiophile world. Overture was recommended to George by Rolly Burnrock. Overture was one of the top audio/video dealers in the world, with one-phone-call-away access to all the top manufacturers and a deep level of expertise among their staff. George found their recommendations to be spot-on.

George lowered the volume on Pete Fountain's Swingin' Blues CD so he could speak with his secretary. "Susan, please get Rolly Burnrock from First Galaxy on the line," asked George. Back up went the volume, just in time for Pete's solo on Muskrat Ramble. Pete Fountain had been George's idol for over 30 years. George loved the sound of Pete's clarinet and made sure the first music he listened to every day was Pete's. George was a huge jazz fan. He still remembered the first jazz concert he ever attended. He was in the 7th grade and saw Pete Fountain at a concert hall in Chicago. George was blown away by Pete's playing and had rarely gone a day without listening to Pete's music since that concert.

The intercom buzzed. "Yes Susan," George said.

"Mr. Burnrock will call you in 15 minutes," Susan reported.

"Thanks," George said, trying to decide what CD to play next. He had recently become a fan of Nelly Furtado after hearing his daughter listening to Nelly's Folklore CD. Nelly Furtado had an enchantingly beautiful voice, deeply moving songs, and an incredible musical talent. Two of his other favorites were Norah Jones and Sonny Rollins. George had recently learned more of Sonny Rollins' story and was amazed at the dedication the tenor sax legend put into his music. In the late 1950's, during a time when he was one of the top three tenor players in the world, Sonny Rollins took several years off from performing so he could "improve his playing." *If only the rest of us had such dedication and high standards*, George thought. *Aw, screw it, it's easier to just listen to his CD's*, and he inserted Way Out West into the CD player, waiting for Mt. St. Rolly to call him back. *I'll keep Nelly Furtado's Folklore CD handy. Track 3 is called 'Explode' and that's probably what Rolly will do when he hears what I have to say.*

Back in Delaware, Rolly Burnrock was preparing to return George's call. He hadn't spoken with George for over a year. As First Galaxy matured, Rolly delegated responsibility for key group relationships to Ted Reilly, his main marketing guy. Rolly wanted to be the decision-maker, not a participant in the day-to-day. However, The Society of Certified Practitioners was one of First Galaxy's oldest and most valuable relationships. SCP represented 10% of First Galaxy's loans and 15% of net income. Plus, First Galaxy was very proud to say that two out of three practicing professionals carried the First Galaxy SCP card. Rolly knew if George was calling him directly, it must be a matter of high importance.

"Rolly, Mr. Kreble is on your line," Helen said through the intercom.

"George! How are you? It's been way too long."

"Hey Rolly. I know what you mean. I guess we get so caught up in the daily stuff that we lose track of time. Things are going great here in Chicago. We're all excited about the Cubs possibly getting to the World Series before the new century is over."

"Yeah, well all we have to worry about here are the Wilmington Blue Rocks. Actually, for a Class AA team, they're pretty damn good. Make sure you give Patti, Harroy and Mollroy my best," said Rolly, passing along his wishes to George's wife and kids. He never did get the reason for having the kids' names end in "roy."

"Thanks Rolly. You've always been a gentleman. I know you're busy so I'll get to the point. We've known been doing business a long time, Rolly, over 10 years. I've got to tell you it seems like First Galaxy is getting soft," George said as he moved the receiver away from his ear, bracing for an 80 decibel blast from Rolly. *Hey DJ! Queue up Explode!*

"What do you mean?" Rolly asked with surprising calm.

"Well, SuiteBanque is kicking your ass out there. I get calls about twice a month from the Production Director at SuiteBanque or some guy at TwoFold Consulting who represents them in some of their marketing efforts. Somehow they know the financial and production arrangements we have with you and they know our contract details. That's a major information leak. I'm pissed that this confidential information has not been protected!" George said.

"You should have told me sooner. This will be addressed immediately. What else is on your mind, George?"

"Well, we've been pretty happy with the SCP credit card program, but SuiteBanque is offering to triple the money we're getting from First Galaxy and they're willing to pay half the contractual money on the day we sign a contract. I'm a strong believer in loyalty, but I would not be doing my job as Chairman if I did not pursue this." *OK, I'll definitely need Explode now.*

"Understood. Clear your calendar for tomorrow. I'm sending Ted Reilly to meet with you and iron this out. Ted will report back directly to me and I will personally deliver our proposal to you. We want to keep your business and help you understand the full picture. I have a favor to ask you, George," Rolly said.

"What's that?" *I guess I took my anticipatory blood pressure pill for nothing. Instead of Explode, I'll listen to In A Mellow Tone.*

"I've been invited to participate in the Summer Economic Summit the President is having at his ranch in Crawford, on the 28th and 29th of June. I would like you to attend with me so we can provide the perspective of your members directly to the President," Rolly said.

"I would be honored to attend with you. Thanks, Rolly. I've never met the President, let alone been to his home. I can't wait to tell Patti," George said.

"Patti is invited too. The evening of the 28th, the President is having a private barbecue at the ranch. You and Patti will be my guests. I'll swing by Chicago on my way and give you a ride. OK. Ted will be at your office 9:00 AM tomorrow, your time. I will be back to you with our proposal within 3 days. Good bye," and without waiting for a response, Rolly disconnected the call, this time without a Richter-scale slam.

"*Bastard!*" Rolly thought to himself as he stood and stormed out of his office.

"Rolly, can I get you something?" Helen asked as she saw The Chairman head off with a volcano-melting look on his face. The only response she heard was the sound of The Chairman's footsteps as he headed in the direction of Ted Reilly's suite.

"June, this is Helen. Red Alert. I believe Rolly is headed your way," Helen said to Ted Reilly's secretary on the phone.

"Thanks, Helen. I'll let Ted… Hello Mr. Burnrock, may I help…"

"Where is Ted?" asked Rolly.

"He's in his conference room with his senior marketing," by the time "room" was out of June's mouth, Rolly was standing in the doorway of Ted Reilly's conference room. He walked in and the executives scurried out as if a light had been turned on in a roach-filled kitchen. They were not used to drop-ins from The Chairman and knew to get the hell out when he entered a room.

Rolly sat next to Ted, sitting so close Ted felt like offering Rolly use of his nose-hair clippers. He noticed a piece of dead skin on Rolly's index finger. Too bad there was nothing handy to clip it off.

"I just got off the phone with George Kreble," Rolly began. "George informed me that we've become soft and that SuiteBanque is, and I quote, kicking our ass. He also was kind enough to let me know that the contractual terms we have with SCP is public information. Oh, and SuiteBanque is offering to triple the money they receive from us."

"I thought something like this might"

"You thought." With that, Rolly went outside the conference room and stared at Ted's name plate outside Ted's office door.

"Rolly, do you want to continue our discussion? Ted asked.

Rolly continued to stare at Ted's name plate. He was so still he made a Buckingham Palace guard look like a break-dancer in comparison.

"What does this say?" Rolly asked.

"It says Ted Reilly," Ted answered.

"Perhaps it should have my name on it **IF I'M GOING TO BE DOING YOUR JOB!** Are you spending time on our *larger* relationships because you clearly have dropped the ball with SCP. Wait, we don't have any larger groups. SCP is our **LARGEST GROUP** and their

Chairman just called to tell ME First Galaxy is about as effective as an eye dropper at a four-alarm fire!"

"Rolly, let's go in and sit down," Ted offered so they could talk in private. "First of all, I asked George to call you. You needed to hear this directly. This is not the first time details about our key relationships have leaked out. Up till now, I've handled it myself. You needed to hear this one because the information is leaking from Sammy Shifster's ex-employees. I'll tell you how I know that in a minute. I need your approval to give Shifster a 2X4 across the head."

"As long as I am Chairman, you will treat Sammy with the respect and loyalty he deserves. You can talk with him about the leaks, but do it in a proper manner."

"One of Shifster's people, a man named Champ Porcer, was a Production Consultant at SPS (Shifster Production Services) after spending 2 years in a similar role at SuiteBanque. Why Shifster would hire someone from our strongest competitor and provide him access to our sensitive information is beyond me. I know Sammy is a master at playing both sides of the street, but now I'm wondering if he's slipping. His recent business decisions wouldn't cut it in a dollar store, let alone the largest credit card bank in the country.

"Anyway, Porcer was recently fired by SPS for trying to get reimbursed for escort service expenses. We have proof that Porcer provided information about our key groups to SuiteBanque while at SPS. We've held off from taking legal action because Porcer is being charged with 28 counts of solicitation of prostitution, bestiality and necrophilia. He was caught in the act in a hospital morgue. If I remember my high school French, 'porcer' is French for 'pig.' Porcer will be in prison a long time if convicted and will need to register as a sex offender if ever released. Yell if you want, but you needed to know about this. Shifster is losing grip and it's got to stop." Ted finished.

"You are going to meet with George tomorrow in his office at 9:00," said Rolly. I want you to learn everything you can about his business situation and how we can help him. We are not losing this group! I told George I would personally present our proposal to him within three days. I also invited him and his wife to the President's Economic Summit in June. Invite him to sit with you in our box at the MLB All-Star game. I have some ideas on how to fix this, and want to hear your recommendation when you return. I'm in town for the next two days, so take my plane to Chicago." Rolly was interrupted with the sound of a child's cry.

"WAAAHHHH. WAAAHHHH. Mine. Mine. Mine. Want it now! Want it now!! Stupid daddy! BUY ME NEW ONE. BUY ME NEW ONE. BUY ME NEW ONE. WAAAHHH." The noises emanated from Topper Penner, Breeze Penner's 3 year old son who was running down the hallway. Topper was wearing a bright red sweater with **BMW OF ASPEN** in bold white letters across the front and **I DRIVE A BEEMER SCOOTER** on the back. Topper and Breeze's wife Winnie had just returned from two months at their house in Wyoming.

"Topper. What's the matter? Tell Uncle Rolly about it," Rolly said as he picked Topper up for a hug.

"Mote troll. Mote troll. Left in Oming. Left in Oming. Daddy dumb." explained Topper.

"He left the remote control to the mini-Ferrari you got him in Wyoming. He has the Ferrari, just not the remote that you had specially built for the car. He's very upset as you can see," Breeze said to Rolly.

"There, there. Uncle Rolly will fix everything," Rolly gently told Topper.

Two hours later, Ted Reilly was in line to purchase a round-trip ticket to Chicago at Philadelphia International Airport. Just about the same time, the First Galaxy jet reached cruising altitude on its way to Wyoming to get Topper's "mote troll."

As soon as Ted got to the gate his cell phone rang. "This is Ted," he answered.

"Where the hell is the *Butts In Seats* report I asked for?" Rolly demanded.

"The one you asked Breeze to get you?" Ted asked, knowing that Rolly was asking to deflect attention from pulling the company jet for 'higher priority business.'

"If I want a smart remark, I'll make it myself. [*one of Rolly's favorite lines from Moe Howard of the Three Stooges*]. If that dipshit LQ wasn't my nephew he'd be shoveling horse shit on a farm somewhere." SLAM went the phone, transforming the Faberge egg from a priceless treasure to a mash of broken glass, loose diamonds and gold decorations. *Why the hell can't some incompetent bastard make a phone you can hang up without damaging antiques!* Rolly thought.

Chapter 7 – The Needy Billionaire

Sammy Shifster was a self-made billionaire who acted like he was yet to earn his first dollar. He thought type-A personalities were too laid back. Sammy believed people existed to work and anyone who did not share his view was a moron. Sammy worked 24/7 and wished there were more hours in the day so more could get done.

Sammy proudly told everyone that annual turnover at his company was 51%. He believed turnover was a motivator since employees were lazy and would only work if they were in fear of losing their job. One year, the turnover rate was only 47% so Sammy got the rate up to 51% by firing his Human Resources director and secretary.

Sammy believed he was a man of impeccable taste: He spent $500 a week on "hair management" to give his hair youthful blond color and a stylishly unkempt look. He fired his personal assistant for failing to place three features of his properties in Agricultural Digest per year. He owned five estates in the United States and a G4 jet, but complained incessantly about having to spend $50 for a backup battery for his cell phone.

Sammy wore custom-tailored Brioni suits with the jackets cut two inches too large in the chest so as not to look "too good" and invite a negotiating opponent to take advantage of him. Sammy owned a store's worth of Brioni's because his weight regularly fluctuated between gaunt and obese, depending on his *Obsession of the Month*. His servant staff had finally figured out the pattern and could predict his wardrobe needs accordingly. Gaunt-causing obsessions included:

- an upcoming Important Palm Beach Social Event

- the need to spend more than $50 on anything other than food
- loss of a coveted business deal
- concern about the possible loss of a coveted business deal
- thinking about future losses of coveted business deals
- worry about whether he really had the largest foyer in Palm Beach because one of his underhanded neighbors might have their foyer expanded at any moment, and
- major panic whenever he would get reports of high morale at Shifster Production Services. This one rarely happened.

Obese-causing obsessions included:
- learning of opportunities to fire staff at SSS
- finding out that an audit of invoices over the past 11 years showed First Galaxy owed him $1,326.83 for marketing services.
- learning that one of his neighbors had built his estate on a former dioxin dump site, and
- those special days when he had back-to-back simultaneous phone calls and face-to-face meetings. Sammy loved a phone in each ear, two speakerphones on the desk and a 48 oz. bag of nachos cheese chips.

Sammy's relationship with First Galaxy had been in place for about 15 years. Sammy's company created and produced custom-made envelopes for First Galaxy's credit card solicitations. Sammy's company, SPS, grew in tandem with First Galaxy as both companies worked together to grow their businesses. SPS provided the production capacity that enabled First Galaxy to mail as many customized credit card solicitations as possible. The more business First Galaxy did, the more money Sammy made. Because SPS received commissions based on business generated from the marketing pieces inside his envelopes, Sammy was constantly pushing First Galaxy to increase the volume of mailings.

As the credit card business became more complex, it was difficult for SPS to deliver the scope and quality of production required by sophisticated customers. High staff turnover and poor hiring decisions at SPS amplified the problem.

Many people at First Galaxy fondly remembered the mid-1990's when SPS had a team of seasoned, professional people. The current SPS crew had the sophistication of Animal House dropouts. Champ "The Pig" Porcer was one of many highly touted hires who were disasters. Champ liked to refer to himself as a "one-man dream team," while people who dealt with him called him the "daily nightmare."

"Good evening, Shifster Production Services, Mr. Shifster's office, this is Elaine."

"Hello. This is Ted Reilly. Is Sammy available?"

"Yes, Mr. Reilly. Mr. Shifster is in the air to Palm Beach. I will transfer you now."

"Ted? Ted? Ted? Hello. Hello. Hello. Ted, you there? **HELLO!!**" Sammy still had not gotten the hang of airplane phones.

"Hello. I'm here. I'm in the air as well, but the connection seems pretty good. We'll have to avoid specifics since we're on airplane phones, but there are a few things we need to discuss," said Ted.

"OK go. How you coming on the marketing plans for next quarter? The stuff I saw was way too low. You guys need to be more aggressive. Why can't you do more mailings? You're only mailing each list six times a year. That leaves six months when some people aren't getting a solicitation," Sammy said.

"That's not what I called about. Your company just dropped a big pile of shit on us and I'm in the process of having it delivered right back to you," Ted knew the only way to get Sammy's attention was to be confrontational.

"I'm listening," said Sammy, who had the listening skills of a Chris Matthews/Bill O'Reilly clone.

"You have some major information security problems, my friend. I've heard from several of our top groups that production and marketing schedules have leaked out to SuiteBanque. That means our biggest competitor knows who we're marketing and when. Do you know what that's going to do to our new business generation this year? I had a stealth audit done at your company and confirmed that controls are lacking and the constant turnover of your staff is encouraging people to violate their confidentiality agreements. I'm on my way to Chicago as we speak to repair the damage this created with our largest relationship. Rolly has a lot of loyalty to you. However, he won't be Chairman forever," Ted laid it out.

"Whatever you need, it's done. I'll put my attorneys on it immediately. It won't happen again. Now what about those ultra-conservative marketing plans?" Sammy persisted.

"Get your head out of your ass! Did you hear anything I said?" Ted answered, trying not to raise his voice on the airplane. "If I really wanted to stick it to SuiteBanque, I'd have you start working for them. Let them deal with your incompetence for a few years and they'll be lucky if they stay in business."

"Well, this is interesting information. I'll get back to you," and Sammy ended the call.

That arrogant, greedy prick, Ted thought. *I know just the way to make his life miserable and solve one of my problems at the same time.* Ted placed a call to his secretary to put his plan in motion.

Chapter 8 – Reaching Out

"Weeeeeeee! Wasn't that a great landing!" Riich squeaked to Vik as their plane touched down in New Orleans for their first *Butts In Seats* visit.

"Yes, Riich. This is exciting. I've never been to New Orleans," Vik replied. *And I've never flown anywhere with someone with breath as bad as yours. Get a mint, loser!*

"I've been here many times. I know the chefs at the major restaurants here. They all love me and are always asking me to sample their new recipes. Did you know I was a guest at the opening of the original Emerald's? His name is Emerald LaFlossie. He's the *BANG!* Guy you've probably seen on TV, books, magazines, the internet, billboards, matchbook ads, grocery stores, and the sides of busses. I'm the one who thought up the *Lift It Up A Notch!* slogan he uses every time he puts seasonings on his food. Can we review our agenda again? Did you reserve a rental car?"

Riich loved to review and re-review his agenda. They had looked at it four times on the flight down.

"Here's another copy Riich. I printed yours on purple paper so it would stand out for you. Our first meeting is at"

"No, what is the agenda for our car, hotel and meals?" Riich interrupted.

"We have a car waiting for us at Gloss Rental, with your Club Platinum Membership. I reserved a Cadillac Escalade, in white pearl, like you asked. We're staying at the Le Centrale Suites, a 5 star hotel in the French Quarter, as you requested. They're a member of the

PlanetStar network so you'll be getting points for both of our rooms through your membership in their Executive Rewards program. The reservations person said this trip will give you enough points to upgrade you to Titanium Level in the rewards program."

"Am I getting an upgraded room for that?" Riich asked.

"Yes, we both get upgraded rooms due to your new Titanium status, since you asked that I have a room adjoining yours."

"Great great great. You did a good job making my arrangements, Vik. That must be my Escalade over there. Let's go."

A porter came over and offered to load their luggage into the car. While leaning over to load the luggage, a $20 bill fell out of the porter's shirt pocket. Riich saw the bill and quickly put his foot over it.

"Heyy. Thankksss so much for loading our luggage, um, uh, Rufus," Riich said, squinting hard to read the man's name tag. "Here's a big tip for you since you did such a great job loading the bags," Riich said and handed the dropped $20 bill back to Rufus. Riich was careful not to touch the man's hand; heaven knew the germs he had picked up from the $20 bill. *He'll probably realize what happened when he's at the liquor store later getting his lottery tickets and cheap wine,* Riich thought. *I just taught him a valuable lesson in protecting your money. It's wonderful the way I'm always helping the little people. I doubt other Senior Executives take the time to be an Educator the way I do.*

Twenty minutes later, they were on I-90 headed downtown. There was a 10 minute delay because Riich could not find his new Michele L'Queen sunglasses. After frantically searching his luggage, he found them in his J'Bancs suit coat pocket.

"That was a very generous tip you gave the porter, Riich." *Did I really just say that?* Victoria thought. *Get it together girl! He's gonna double-charge the bank for the tip anyway.*

"Well, that's what I do. They're people too, you know. Make a note of the tip so I can, I mean for when you put it on the expense report."

As they got on the exit for Poydras Street, Riich saw a large high school. "Hey, Vik, there's a high school. Get the name of it so I can do some Outreach there."

Continuing on Poydras Street, Riich turned left onto Carondolet. When he got to the intersection with Canal Street, he stopped suddenly. "Vik, hand me my cell. Thannkksss. Show me the phone number of the hotel. What was the name again? Thannkkksss.

"Helllooo. This is Riichard Shunk, a Senior Executive at First Galaxy. I am in town for several important meetings at First Galaxy's offices here and..... what? First G a l a x y. Astronomy? No, I'm not looking for the aquarium. I am a Senior Executive at First Galaxy BANK. I have just traveled all the way from Philadelphia, Pennsylvania and I need you to confirm the directions to your hotel, um Le Centrale Suites.

"My location? Vik, where are we? Thannkkksss. No, not you, I'm thanking the person with me. We're at the corner of Canal and Bourbon Streets. OK. We'll be there to check-in in a few minutes. Thannkkksssssss.

"That's weird. I've been to New Orleans many times and was part of the Senior Executive team that flew down on the First Galaxy Jet when the New Orleans office was opened, but this intersection must have been reconfigured. That's why I called to get directions. No need to panic, Vik. We'll be there in a minute."

They pulled up to the Le Centrale entrance five minutes later. Riich led the way to guest reception as the bell captain unloaded the Escalade. Riich was so excited to arrive that he forgot to tip the Doorman, so Victoria gave him $5.00 of her own money.

"Helllooo. Mr. Riichard Shunk. Senior Executive with First Galaxy. First Galaxy BANK. Checking in. You are supposed to have my Platinum Premier Executive Exclusive Rewards Program number already entered?"

"Oh yes. You're the Astronomer from Pittsburgh I just spoke with on the phone. You made good time, sir. Some of our streets can be so tricky when you haven't been here before. Welcome to Le Centrale, Mr. Shunk. Did you and your daughter have a pleasant trip?" asked the Guest Reception Specialist.

"This isn't my daughter. My daughter is on the honor roll at Private Preparatory Academy and constantly gets phone calls from Major Universities offering full scholarships. I am in a hurry as I have several important meetings this afternoon. Is my suite ready?"

Victoria forced herself to keep a blank face after Riich's insult. *What a pile he is*, she thought. *He's got less class than fat women who wear speedo suits at the beach.*

"Forgive me, Mr. Shunk. Your suites are ready and we have your Platinum Premier Executive Exclusive Rewards Program information credited. Congratulations on reaching Titanium status with us. You are in the Platinum Magnolia Suite and Ms. Cummins is in the Titanium Mint Julep Suite. The elevators are"

"Excuuse mee," Riich interrupted. "You must have made a mistake. I am the one with Titanium status. Shouldn't *I* be in the Titanium Suite?"

"A very good observation, Mr. Shunk. I've always heard that people from Pittsburgh are very sharp and you certainly fit the bill. Both suites are comparable, but yours has a better view of the French Quarter. If you would like, we can change the plates on the doors to reflect that you are in the Titanium Mint Julep Suite. The elevators are directly to your right. The Bell Captain will be up shortly with your luggage. My name is Bradley. Please enjoy your stay in New Orleans and if there is anything I can do for you, just give me a jingle."

"Yes, I want the plates changed. Thannkkksssss." The hiss of the sssss hung in the air as Riichard rounded the corner to the elevators, moving like he had just found out the winning powerball ticket was inside the elevator.

When the Bell Captain arrived with their luggage, Riich tipped him $5.00. Five minutes later, Victoria heard a tap-tap-tap-tap-tap on the adjoining doors to their suites.

"Hey there!! How ARE you? Remember to write out an expense ticket for the $20 tip I just gave to the Bellman. Is your suite as sweet as mine? I got a big bottle of champagne, a fruit basket and flower arrangement as a Titanium status welcome gift. Oh, I see you just got a fruit basket. I'll call down and have them bring up more gifts if you want. Your suite is almost as big as mine but I do have a better view of The Quarter; that's what the locals call it. I just got off the phone with my wife. We must have been talking for half an hour. She was very glad to know I arrived safely and said the kids are really sad that

I'm away and they miss me very much because we're all so close and we're really more like friends than parent and children. I'm just going to leave my adjoining door open most of the time if you want to leave yours open. I need to go out to pick up a few things. I'll be back later to have drinks before dinner. Don't worry about figuring out what to order, I can do that for you since I'm a wine expert and a gourmet. Gotta run. Thankkkssss."

"Hellooo. Is Bradley available? Hi Bradley, this is Riichard in the Titanium Suite, you know, the one that's having the name plates changed? I did not receive my welcome gifts and would like them brought to my suite now. Thannnkkkssss." Riich would need to make his next phone call from a pay phone. He pulled a crumpled piece of paper from his pocket. It had the phone number of the cocaine source recommended to Riich by one of his friends in Delaware. *Shoot! I should have told the desk clerk to send me up some quarters.*

In the next room, Victoria was also placing a call. "Hi, I'm calling on behalf of Mr. Shunk. Please send up two bottles of your best white wine, assorted cold cuts, some bags of those honey-coated peanuts and other snacks, and a pound of caviar to the Platinum Magnolia Suite. Mr. Shunk would like it sent up as soon as possible and said to add a 30% tip." *Thank you, Riich for teaching me so much about 'leadership',* Victoria thought. *I'm gonna chill here awhile, then hit Pat O'Briens. I've gotta make sure I'm not here when the dork returns for dinner.*

The next morning, Riichard and Victoria arrived at First Galaxy's "Bayou Building" at 7:45 to do the *Butts In Seats* greetings.

"Missed you last night, Vik. I knocked on your door for dinner, but you didn't answer." Riich said.

"Oh, sorry, Riich. I don't have a lot of travel experience like you and I was so exhausted from the trip that I fell asleep real early. I must have been sleeping so deeply that I didn't hear you knock. I wanted to get a good rest so I'd be ready to tally your greetings today." *Thank goodness I didn't eat breakfast yet, or I would have just made myself heave*, thought Victoria.

"This is like going home for me, Vik. I've been here so many times and the employees here love me. They always ask me to stay and become the Managing Executive at this site. I should have allowed more time to be here since I'll be stopped by so many employees wanting to talk with me."

"Good moorrnnning! How ARE you? Great to see you." Riich announced to the security guard at the front entrance.

"Your name, sir?" the guard asked.

"I am Riichard Shunk, Senior Executive, here from Delaware for a series of important meetings."

"What company are you with, Mr. Chunk?" the guard asked.

"It's Shunk; s h u n k. I am with First Galaxy and am a Senior Executive. Please open the door so I will not be late for my important meetings," Riich demanded.

"Riich, show him your badge and he'll let us in," Victoria suggested, as she showed the guard her badge.

"You forgot to remind me to bring it, Vik," Riich snapped.

You forgot to flush your head down the toilet, LOSER!, Victoria thought.

"Mr. Shunk, may I please have your manager's name so I can contact him to confirm your status?" the guard asked.

"David Gando, but I was hired directly by the Chairman, Mr. Burnrock. You've probably never met him. I see him all the time at Senior Executive meetings and events and he invites me to his home for important social gatherings and usually asks for my recommendations on wine selection. You can call Mr. Burnrock if David is not available." Riich replied.

A few minutes later, the guard passed the phone to Riich. "Mr. Gando would like to speak with you, Mr. Shunk."

"Heyy there, Dave. How ARE you? What? I am at our Bayou Office. Why am I here? I am here to visit the Banks in the area to talk with them about um expanding yeah expanding the um marketing we're doing. You didn't know about the trip? I gave my secretary Victoria the itinerary memo to hand deliver to you. I will speak with her about her mistake. What? Did I drop Mr. Burnrock's name to try to get in? That's a funny one, Dave. The security clerk must have been confused because I said I was in town to meet with *local* bank presidents and he must have thought I meant *our* bank president. Anyway, I've got a very full schedule of important meetings with the local bank presidents, like I just told you. I'll pass you back to the security clerk. Thankkksssssss."

A few minutes later, Riich was inside with a large Guest Pass badge pasted on his J'Bancs suit coat. "It would be a lot more efficient if they let Senior Executives go through their own entrance. You can tell that security clerk is not used to dealing with high level people. Mr. Burnrock would be very upset if he knew I had to go through all of this to get into my own building. Hurry up to the café or I will miss my chance to do today's greetings," Riich said while searching for the café. "They moved the café since the last time I was here. Remember to keep a tally of the greetings I do."

"Just try not to do them so fast that I can't keep up with you, Riich! Especially since you know so many people here." Victoria said while imagining Riich slipping on a banana peel and sliding head first into the café like a bowling ball.

They finally found the cafe and Riich began his greetings.

"Good moorrnnning! How ARE you? Great to see you."

"Good moorrnnning! How ARE you?"

"Good moorrnnning! How ARE you? Great to see you."

"Good moorrnnning! How ARE you?"

"Good moorrnnning! How ARE you? Great to see you."

One employee had the nerve to respond to Riich's greeting by actually starting to tell him how she was. He dismissed her with a quick "Gotta run, thannkkksss" before returning to his greetings. Riich explained to Vik that it would not be fair for the other clerks to miss their greeting because one employee monopolized his time. After 10 minutes, Riich had enough and walked towards the entrance, greeting everyone he passed with "Good moorrnnning! How's evvvreeethinggggg?" as he proceeded at a fast executive pace.

"That was just super! Did you see how happy everyone was to see me? Make sure you get the *Butts In Seats* report from yesterday – no, get it from yesterday and from last Wednesday and whichever is lower I'll use as the benchmark. We should see it go up in the next few days. Get on the distribution list for the report so you can monitor it going forward. All increases will be due to my efforts, just like at headquarters.

"Hey, Vik, which did you like better, 'Good moorrnnning! How ARE you?' or

'Good moorrnnning! How ARE you? *Great to see you.*' I alternated them to keep it fresh. I like it with the 'Great to see you' tacked on since I've been here so many times before and everyone here knows me."

"They both sounded good, Riich," Vik answered. *GAG!! I know Evangelical Used Car Salesmen with more sincerity than this loser. I must have blinked my eyes when 'all the people who know him' were around because he's about as well known in this building as a refugee from a Mongolian prison camp.*

"Do you have the totals? Riich asked.

"Totals?"

"I asked you to keep a tally of the greetings."

"Yes, I'm sorry. You did 23 greetings this morning." Victoria tallied 27 greetings, but deducted a few for entertainment.

"Are you sure? Only 23? It was that clerk that stopped to talk with me that slowed me down. That was worth 4 greetings alone. And we arrived late since you did not remind me to bring my badge. You probably missed counting some since this is all so new to you and you were probably overwhelmed. And there are fewer employees at this site than at Global HQ so if you normalize the number of greetings for the difference in the number of employees and adjust for the ones you missed, I really did 48 greetings. 48! A new record! Isn't that exciting, Vik!

"Did you get the name of the high school we passed yesterday? I'm going to do some Outreach after I drop you at the hotel." Riich said.

"Yes, it's New Orleans High School." *You can tell by the sign on the front of the school, dipshit.*

"Great. Let's go. It's almost lunch time."

Riich dropped Vik back at the hotel and headed to New Orleans High School. It was almost 10:30, so he would definitely be on time for the lunch break. He parked the Escalade in the Steak-Ums Good Food Fast parking lot across the street from the school. Riich made sure he parked parallel to the school so he could be seen sitting in the Escalade as kids approached from the school. *"Shouldn't be long now,"* he thought to himself, tuning the radio to a hip-hop station and turning the volume up, to get the fenders vibrating.

At 11:00 a bell sounded and kids started pouring out the doors. *Shit. There are a ton of black kids here. Aren't there any white kids? This looks like a nice neighborhood,* Riich thought. After 15 minutes, Riich saw what he was looking for: some whites heading towards the Escalade.

"Hey there!" Riich said to the first one. "Where do you go to party around here?"

"Up yours, asshole," the kid said and kept walking.

"Hey there!" Riich said to the next one. "Where do you go to party around here?"

"At your crib when you not there, bitch."

"Hey there!" Riich said to the next kid. "Where do you go to party around here?"

"With your mama," the kid said, continuing on his way.

"Hey there!" Riich crooned to a girl who walked by. "Where do you go to party around here?"

"Encima de su perdedor del asno!" the girl said and kept walking.

"Does that mean 'yes'?" Riich called out hopefully.

"Hey there!" Riich said again. "Where do you go to party around here?"

"What kind of party you talking about?" asked a kid in patched up jeans and Swollen Members 2002 World Tour t-shirt. Riich liked the kid's long black hair and thin frame.

"Whatever kind you like. I got some party supplies in my Escalade. You want to see?" Riich said, telling himself not to get so excited.

"Um... I don't know. I'm hooking up with my girlfriend for lunch."

"That's cool. She can come. Does she like to party?"

"Yeah. You got any coke? That's what I like. Some cognac would be good too," the boy said.

"I got you covered, my friend. Got the coke right here and we can go get the cognac. I'm Riich. What's your name?"

"My name's... Yo Susie! Over here!" the kid called out after seeing his girlfriend walk out of the school. Susie looked extra hot today in pink low-riders, tight sweater and her brown hair pulled back into a ponytail.

"Hey Chris. What's up?" Susie said as she walked over.

"This is.... What's your name again?"

"Riich."

"This is Riich. You wanna go party with him? He's got some glad stuff and he's gonna get us some cognac. Let's go get amped." Chris said.

"Yeah, I could use some kick back time. All my classes today are a bunch of gomers anyway. So, you got some wacky dust, daddy?" Susie said.

"I got you covered, um… Susan. Chris and I were sitting here rapping and just, you know, like, waiting for you to show. You wanna stop and get some tunes on the way cause me and Chris were"

"Zip up and let's go. We got to be back here by 3 to get the bus." Chris cut in. *Load me up so I can't hear this moron anymore,* thought Chris.

Four hours later, Riich brought Chris and Susie back to school. The kids got out and ran toward the bus lot.

"Damn! I am cooked! I better get a shot of shock or my old lady's gonna give me the leather." Chris said to Susie.

"Where did you find that creep, Chris? What a perv. Ok, so he took us to some sleaze Snow Motel. That's a price for the blow. Didn't you get creeped out by him?"

"Shit. I was so wasted I didn't even know what was going on!" Chris said as the color drained from his face.

"You were pounding the dust so fast that you blacked out." Susie then told Chris what happened after he blacked out.

"Shut up. I'm gonna heave. I gotta get home and take a shower. Please believe me, Susie, I don't remember any of this!" Chris said and ran over to some bushes and spewed. I'm cutting back on the blow after this. You should too."

"Oh, of course, doctor. Save the death-bed conversion bullshit for someone else, or for your next boyfriend!" and Susie ran off, sobbing and shaking.

Cold bitch, Chris thought. *I've gotta get a shower. Mom will freak if she sees me; I guess it's good she's never around. I should skate by on this.*

Chris' mom Maria worked an 11AM-7PM shift at the local All-Store MegaCenter, six days a week. She liked to stop at a bar on the way home to "take the edge off." New Orleans was filled with business travelers so Maria rarely drank alone. A few times each month she'd spend the night with her new friend. Maria filled her dresses a little more than she used to, but her curves and warm smile were still good enough to get the eye of most men. It wasn't easy for a single mother in her early 40's to develop a good relationship, so Maria met her needs one night at a time. She felt a little guilty leaving Chris home alone, but it was only a few nights a month and he was 17 and old enough to watch out for himself. Besides, he kept himself locked in his room and didn't even know if she was there or not.

Maria got home around 8:30. It was a slow night at The Big E-Z Pub and she was tired. She couldn't wait to get out of her tight skirt. The house was dark and smelled faintly of alcohol, sweat and vomit.

"Chris! I'm home." Maria called out. No answer. Maria turned on some lights and walked down to Chris' room. The door was open and Chris was passed out on his bed, wearing a clean tee-shirt and underwear. Maria looked in the bathroom adjacent to Chris' room and saw the shower was wet, the floor was wet and the toilet was splattered with vomit. The surprising thing was there were no clothes or towels on the floor. Chris always threw that stuff on the floor and would only take the load down to be washed after the pile got so high that his head banged the ceiling.

Maria was about to wake Chris up when she remembered the red blinking light on the answering machine. *Probably another ad from SkinFlint Mortgage or Tin Can Mobile Phones*, Maria thought as she pushed the play button.

"This is Ms. Oxgrod, Senior Assistant Guidance Counselor at New Orleans High School. This message is for… um…. Maria Jeffish. Your child, Christopher left school today at the 11:00 lunch period and did not return. This is the seventh truancy occurrence in the past month. Even though he is maintaining the state-mandated 'D' average, his teachers have informed me that he is in jeopardy of losing his eligibility for after-school programs if his grades slip. As this would impact the level of funding our school receives from the state, we are quite concerned as you can imagine. Please call me at 530-0202 so I may discuss this with you. I have already left

several messages on your machine,
but you have not returned my calls.
Per school district policy, after I
have left five more messages, I will
follow up with a letter sent to your
address by registered mail. Thank
you."

"Chris! Chris! Wake Up!" Maria shouted as she ran to Chris' room. "Chris! Listen to me! Get up!" Maria yelled as she ran into Chris' room and turned the light on.

Chris did not move.

Maria gently shook him, but he did not wake up. The sheets were soaked with sweat. Maria's pulse quickened and she put a palm on Chris' forehead. It was cool and clammy. His hair was damp and matted. His skin was ghost white. Maria continued to try to awaken Chris. He finally made a groaning noise and opened his eyes, but his eyeballs were rolling back. Maria squeezed Chris' hand and it felt clammy and lifeless. "Hold on baby, I'm going to get some help." Maria said as she picked up the phone and called 911.

When the paramedics arrived, they saw the all too familiar signs of drug and alcohol over-use. Another teenager turning the promise of a bright future into a drug-poisoned death trap. They assured Maria that her son would be ok, but that he needed to go to the hospital for treatment.

After a three hour wait in the emergency room, a doctor explained to Maria that Chris had consumed dangerous amounts of cocaine and alcohol, and that based on examination of his nasal passages and a liver scan, he was a regular drug and alcohol user. He said that Chris would be required to enter a substance abuse treatment program immediately after release from the hospital. The doctor said a police officer would be out to speak with her shortly.

"Thank you, doctor. I am so sorry... I had no idea this was going on. Please let the police officer know I am waiting for him." Maria said, and bowed her head to pray for help.

Chapter 9 – All For One

"OK, Reed. That's a great idea. Go ahead and handle it the way you suggested. I'll see you at lunch," said Tom Hughman as he ended a phone call with Ted Reilly.

"Joanna, please get Wallace Malvagio on the phone for me," Tom asked his secretary. Tom was about to follow-up on the Chairman's question regarding Wallace's expense reduction memo.

"He's on the line, Tom," said Joanna.

"Thanks. I'll pick it up in a minute.

"Wallace. Hello. I hope the house expansion is coming along good. I hear you're adding three rooms, an olympic size pool and a golf green. Must be a lot of money to do all that. The Chairman was very interested your expense reduction memo."

"Good. Maybe some fat will finally be cut. This is only a start. There's more to do," Wallace replied.

"I know you like numbers Wallace, and I have some here I was reviewing. You have 75,000 stock options with a strike price of $4.50 expiring in 7 days. Based on First Galaxy's current stock price of $33 that would be a profit to you of $2.1 million. Of course, it would also be an expense to the company of $2.1 million. To help with the expense reductions you proposed to the Chairman, I went ahead and cancelled the 75,000 stock options and will instead issue you 25,000 new options with a strike price of $40. That way, you reduce expenses now while benefiting from the increased future value of the company. Great work, Class. I'll be sure to update the Chairman," and Tom hung up the phone.

Chapter 10 – Lashin' Into It

Barney O'Farkle was in a big hurry. He was moving so fast his huge gut bounced up and down like a water balloon. His shirt, stretched so tight that it met military bed sheet standards, had come completely un-tucked from his pants. None of this mattered to a man who wore the same suit 3-4 days in a row, with the same belt loop missed on his pants.

"Hwarya! Hwarya! Hwarya!" Barney may have been in a hurry, but he still said "how are you" to each employee he passed. Barney believed it was important to acknowledge the underlings when he passed them in the hallway. He had learned to be polite to the servant staff from his father.

Barney burst into his department, moving so fast the papers on Sally's desk blew onto the floor. A 5'7" 265 lbs. man creates a lot of wind. He had just returned from a very important meeting with Ted Reilly.

"**SILLEEE!** Give amma um amma Inside Movers a shout. I'm movin to the amma amma amma Production Division. It's right from the mouth of Ted Reilly. He wants me lashin into me new job right away. Said its an amma amma amma top-of-the-list priority. I just got out of a meetin with Ted Reilly. He said the lads in Production and at SPS need me leadership to get all the spurs in the saddles, ya know! Ted wants me to give Stanley Spinner a shout right off to set up a meetin with him. Give Stanley a shout soon as you get the Movers done and dusted."

Ted Reilly had just told Barney that he would be leaving Special Situations and moving to Production. Ted indicated that Production was adrift and he wanted Barney to fire up the SPS people and be joined at the hip with Sammy Shifster. Ted wanted Barney in constant communication with Sammy and his staff and have real-time knowledge on the status of all Production activities. Barney did not need to learn about the production process. Ted wanted him to be an Administrator and keep everything moving along. "Give Sammy a call right away, he'll be very glad to hear from you," were Ted's parting words to Barney.

"Sillee, give Stanley Spinner a shout so I can talk to the lad, ya know!" Barney asked Sally.

"OK, Barney. I spoke with Internal Movement and they will be here to move your stuff today. You will be in your new location tomorrow," said Sally. *Please, please don't take me with you,* Sally thought while crossing both sets of fingers. She had been with Barney for two years and was fed up with his aphorisms, thoughtlessness and arrogance, all concealed in a happy-go-lucky façade. Unfortunately for Sally, First Galaxy had a policy that Senior Executives could take their secretaries with them when they changed jobs, so she was at his mercy.

"Mr. Shifster is on your line, Barney."

"Amma amma amma amma amma."

"Who the hell is Emma!" Sammy demanded. "This is Sammy Shifster. I thought there was a Barney O'Farkle on the line!"

"Amma amma wut-wuz-I-gonna-say-to-ya um yes um this is Barney O'Farkle of First.. Second am First Galaxy. I amma wanted to speak to Stanley Spinner of PSP, ya know. Ted Reilly told me to give him a shout," Barney explained to the person on the phone.

"You mean me, Sammy Shifster. I know Ted. Who is this? said Sammy.

"Amma it's Barney O'Farkle, Sammy. Me secretary gave me the wrong amma name. I'm gettin settled into me new role as Production Director and Ted asked me to amma set up a meetin with you and your ammmmmm staff to go over some reports and schedule some more meetins, ya know!"

"What reports? I don't look at reports. Get to the point."

"Amma amma amma amma amma." Before the 6th "amma" could come out, Sammy had hung up the phone.

Chapter 11 – Play My Song

Two times a year, Rolly had a special version of the Morning Management Meeting (SMMM), for all Senior Executives, which included the rank of Executive Deputy President and above. The meeting was held in a First Galaxy House Of Cards, specially built auditoriums where First Galaxy and community organizations could hold meetings for up to 500 people. First Galaxy had a House Of Cards at each of its sites.

There were over 200 Senior Executives attending the SMMM. The parking lot looked like a Mercedes dealership on steroids. There were so many black "S" Class Benz's in one place that the Philadelphia Carjacking Society had issued a "Jack-Off Alert" to its members.

There were more injuries at an SMMM than an NFL game. With 200 Important Executives doing the big arm swoop to check their watches, the person sitting to the left of the Important Executive, (an Important Executive him or herself) often received a severe jab in the eye socket bone, resulting in a fracture or black eye. These Executives were accustomed to sitting in spacious offices and conference rooms where they could do their arm swoops in front of an audience of low-level employees, not in cramped move-theater auditorium seats used by civilians. Worst of all, there was no audience to impress with their importance!

More contact lenses and eyeglasses were damaged during this event than any other time of the year. This was a boon to L`Optique Boutique, a local high-end optical store. On the day of each SMMM,

L`Optique Boutique offered emergency replacement of 24-karat gold glass frames and custom-colored contact lenses.

Rolly could sense that his executives were getting bored, since the frequency of arm swoops was increasing. They needed to get back to their departments to regain their sense of self-importance. He wanted to wrap up the meeting with a discussion of *Butts In Seats.*

"We look at *Butts In Seats* every day, a key measure of your success in motivating and inspiring your employees. There has been significant room for improvement at all of our sites so far this year, with the exception of Global HQ. I am pleased to report that *Butts In Seats* has recently returned to targeted levels throughout the company and have asked Breeze Penner to give an update on how this was achieved."

"Thank YOU Mr. Chairman! We put a whole bunch of initiatives in place over the past month to make *Butts In Seats* better and each one has delivered superior results. Every idea we implemented worked in spectacular fashion. Actual results far exceeded the highest end of our expectations. This was a success unrivaled by any other initiative put in place during the past month! What an outstanding, unbelievable, incredible job we did! Let's give ourselves a big round of applause for our amazing accomplishments! COME ON!! 1 2 3! WE LOVE FIRST GALAXY!!!! YEAH!!" As often happened, Breeze got so wound up that he forgot the latest 'spectacular success' and 'unrivaled accomplishment' he was talking about and went into full-on cheerleader mode. Tom Hughman walked up to Breeze, and with a big smile on his face and a vise-like grip on the back of Breeze's neck, whispered to Breeze, "Cut the crap, LQ, or Rolly is going to have you run over by a garbage truck. *Butts In Seats*!! Remember!" "Oh yeah. Thanks Alps." Breeze replied, genuinely touched that Tom had helped him out.

"We conducted a survey to learn employee awareness of *Butts In Seats*, we offered $0.05 off coffee in the cafes on random days, we put up posters celebrating the importance of *Butts In Seats* and...."

"Excuuse mee. Excuuse meee."

"Yes. Your name please," Breeze said.

"Helllooo. How ARE you? I am Riichard Shunk, Executive Deputy President, with First Galaxy 14 years and I have had 35 jobs here. Like the Chairman, I have been concerned about *Butts In Seats*. As an involved Leader, I decided to take matters into my own hands and over the past few weeks have visited every First Galaxy site to greet the employees. I have been doing these greetings here every day for 14 years and now that I have done them at the other sites, *Butts In Seats* has gone up all across First Galaxy. I sent the Chairman, Ted and Tom a little update on my visits, but it must have gotten lost. I know each of you are as proud as I am that *Butts In Seats* is now above target," Riich said proudly as he flashed a winning smile, looked all around the room, and sat down.

"Well done... there," Rolly boomed. "It's about time someone showed some initiative around here. We need more leaders like... you who are involved in the business and don't wait to be asked to do something."

"I second the Chairman's remarks," said Ted Reilly. "Richard is also doing a great job keeping his employees pumped up. Just a week or two ago I walked past a conference room at 6:30 and his staff was working away. Great leadership, Richard. Thank you."

Wow, Riich thought. *I'm even more impacting than I thought. Look how in awe of me everyone is. Whenever there is complete silence, I know that means the group is happy for me and loves me.*

After the meeting, Rolly asked Ted Reilly to meet him in his office.

"I was very impressed by that boy, Richard Shunk. What level is he?" Rolly asked.

"He's an Executive Deputy President."

"Promote him to Senior Executive Deputy President. We need executives like that who inject energy, sincerity and passion into the business. Let Tom know I want a new Morale Enhancement position created in Personnel and that Richard will be the director."

"Rolly, before we make a decision on this, I think..."

"One more thing. I have a message to call George Kreble. What do you think that's about?"

Ted's meeting with George had gone well. Ted walked George through a history of the business relationship and SCP's growth during its partnership with First Galaxy. Ted presented detailed customer satisfaction results showing that SCP members rated the First Galaxy card very high for utility, reliability and service. More than 50% of SCP members said they would continue to use the card even if it did not have the SCP logo on it. SCP customers rated the quality and creativity of the marketing and account information pieces they received as best-in-class. Per the SCP contract, all production was done by First Galaxy, not SPS.

George was impressed with Ted's presentation and his commitment to the relationship by visiting in person. He was still very excited about Rolly's invitation to the President's Economic Summit. Ted invited George to the MLB All Star Game, with seats right behind the 3rd base dugout. George understood the not-so-subtle message that First Galaxy provided access and services no other card issuer could provide. However, he still had a major financial gap between SuiteBanque's offer and the money he was earning from First Galaxy.

The meeting ended cordially. As a thank you to Ted and Rolly, George gave each of them an Apple iPod, pre-loaded with all of Pete Fountain's recordings. Ted and George agreed to meet again in 2 days to discuss First Galaxy's proposal.

After Ted debriefed Rolly on his meeting with George, Rolly laid out First Galaxy's proposal. Rolly and Ted flew to Chicago the next day to present the proposal to George.

"George. Thank you for meeting with us. Here is our proposal," Rolly said and handed George a leather-bound portfolio in SCP colors, with the SCP and First Galaxy logos on the cover. Inside was one sheet of gold-leaf bond paper detailing the proposal.

"George, we've been partners a long time and I want our partnership to continue. If you're main interest is a big check, you should sign with SuiteBanque today. We don't believe in buying partnerships, we like to earn them through relationships that are mutually beneficial.

"We are offering you the opportunity to earn more money by increasing the amount we pay you, and by expanding the suite of products you endorse. In return for higher royalties, we want to expand our relationship to include practice financing, auto leasing, mortgage lending and other products of interest to your members. We also want to extend the contract term for 10 years. In other words, First Galaxy will be your primary financial services provider. No other bank is positioned to deliver this depth of product line to you. This is a very generous, fair and balanced offer. What is your answer?" Rolly asked.

"Well, Rolly. This is a very robust proposal. I'd like some time to"

"The offer expires when I leave your office today. By the way, that's a beautiful hi-fi system over there. I see you took my recommendation and went with Overture. I need to use the restroom. That will give you enough time to decide," Rolly said as he left the room.

"Jesus, Ted," George said to Ted after Rolly stepped out. I need more time to review your offer."

"More time won't change our offer. This is pretty basic, George. You can choose to stay with a partner who has exceeded your needs for over 10 years, or you can subject your members to all the turmoil that comes from changing issuers, in return for one large royalty check," Ted said.

"I want my iPod back, you prick," George said with a laugh. "I'm going to use the restroom too since I just shit my pants."

Rolly returned to George's office. "Where is he?" Rolly asked Ted.

"Using the restroom. I think we're in good shape."

George returned to his office and offered to put on some music.

"The only song I want to hear is 'I Accept Your Offer' by George Kreble," Rolly said, in a rare display of humor.

"OK, you son of a bitch. I accept. You're right. This is a great offer and a great partnership. Ted sealed it when he showed me the customer survey results the other day. I greatly appreciate both of you coming out to discuss it with me in person. Now I can tell my Board that I brought the Evil Bankers to their knees."

And with that, all had a good laugh and shook hands. George and Rolly signed the proposal sheet and Ted was to follow up with the formal contract.

"I'm not sure why George is calling. Do you want to call him now while I'm here?" Ted replied to Rolly's question.

"Helen. Get George Kreble on the phone, please."

"OK Rolly. Go ahead," Helen said.

"George. I've got you on speaker. Ted is here with me."

"Hello George."

"Hello, gentlemen. Thanks for calling back. Are you behind closed doors?" George asked.

"No, why?" Rolly replied.

"I have something rather sensitive to tell you and since you're on a speakerphone, I don't think you'll want anyone to hear it," George said.

"Alright, the door is closed."

"This is awkward. A few weeks ago, there was an article in the local paper about drug use by high school kids. The article said that a lot of adults are using the lure of drugs to hook up with kids. There was an example of several kids at Lake Michigan High School, the one near your Chicago site, being asked if they wanted to "party" by a middle-aged man in some type of fancy SUV.

"Well, I didn't think anymore about it, because that seems to be the sick world we're in. But today, there was a follow-up article. It said the same man had been parked by the school for three days in a row. One of the kids' parents saw that her kid was high when he got home from school and took him right back to the school to talk with the Principal. The kid said he and his girlfriend had gotten some cocaine from a guy parked across the street from the school at lunchtime. The kid said the man had a First Galaxy badge on his pants and some First Galaxy binders on the back seat. He recognized the logo after seeing a First Galaxy commercial on TV. The police are planning an investigation. I wanted to give you a heads-up. Sorry for being the messenger of bad news, but I thought you would want to know."

"You're a good friend George. Thank you for calling," Rolly said and hung up.

"Get Special Security Investigations on this immediately," said Rolly. "Find out why the moron running our Chicago office didn't alert us. Get me a copy of those articles. Someone is impersonating a First Galaxy employee. We've got to find out who this perverted pile of shit is."

Chapter 12 – An Abundance Of Talent

Once a month, Rolly devoted his Morning Management Meeting to a review of recent letters from First Galaxy Customers. He believed it was important to stay focused on issues of concern to the Customer. Rolly had a random sample of 100 letters pulled for discussion.

"OK, next letter," Rolly said at the midway point of the meeting.

"This one is from a Customer who recently had some difficulty paying his bills on time," said Tom Hughman.

Dear Mr. Burnrock,

I was laid off from my job earlier this year and as a result, had difficulty paying my bills, including my First Galaxy account. I was about two months behind on your account when I received a phone call from Mr. Mark Ruttle of your Special Situations department. At first I was stunned by Mr. Ruttle's politeness and empathy. After we spoke for a few minutes, I realized he was sincerely interested in helping me out. I received numerous calls from collectors who threatened and belittled me, but First Galaxy and Mr. Ruttle are different.

Mark stayed in regular contact with me. As it turned out, I got back on my feet and was able to resume payments on my own. However, Mark was prepared to offer me a special program if I had needed it. Yours is the only company that treated me with respect and showed that you valued my business.

I'm enjoying more career and financial success than ever, thanks to a new product launch. I will always be a loyal First Galaxy Customer and encourage my friends to do business with you. Please thank Mr. Ruttle for the great way he represents First Galaxy.

Sincerely,
Alan Moore
President, Gibraltar Metal Products

"What do you think?" Rolly asked Tom.

"It's great to hear. It shows that treating people with respect is the right thing to do and is smart business. I'd like to ask Mark Ruttle to stop by so we can thank him together," Tom replied.

"Who is the director of Special Situations?" Rolly asked.

"It was Barney O'Farkle until last week. Barney is now our Production Director," Tom said.

"Helen, contact Mark Ruttle and Barney O'Farkle and ask them to come to my office right away," Rolly said.

"Alright, let's continue reviewing letters until they get here."

A few minutes later, the sound of "Hwarya" grew in volume, indicating that Barney had arrived. He entered Rolly's office with Mark Ruttle following. Rolly and his executives stood up to greet Mark.

"Mark, we just finished reading a letter of commendation for your efforts with Alan Moore. I want to congratulate you for representing First Galaxy in a superior manner. He was very generous in his praise of you and the way you handled his situation," Rolly said.

"Thank you, Mr. Burnrock. I worked with my" Mark started.

"Yes. Yes. It's absolutely phenomenal," Barney interrupted. "I was in on all the meetins about amma wut-wuz-his-name amma Mr. Marks. I gave ammm… Mark here the guidance to handle this late payin business and all, ya know! I gave me approval to offer the ummma wut-is-it-called-again amma amma special accounting terms and told Mark to make sure the collectin of those finance charges and late fees was done and dust…"

"I'm sorry, what were you saying, Mark," Tom Hughman jumped in.

"I just wanted to thank you, Mr. Burnrock, and Mr. Reilly for inviting me in and for showing me the letter. I appreciate the opportunity to help our Customers," Mark said.

"We're proud of you Mark. We won't keep you any longer. Thanks," said Tom. Each of the executives shook Mark's hand and he returned to his department.

"Barney, I hear you're our new Production Director," said Rolly.

"Yes yes. I'm over the moon about it, ya know. I've been busier than a one armed paper hanger. I've been lashin into the reports and settin up meetins about all the stuff, ya know! Me and amma amma amma amma Sammy Shif… Shiffff…. amma Shifster are joined at the hip and digging into all the deals. I've got all his phone numbers in me office phone and havin them put into my amma amma wireless too, ya know."

"Barney is the right man for the job. Keep things moving, Barney. See you later," Ted said to get Barney the hell out of Rolly's office.

"He's got a lot of enthusiasm," said Rolly. "He's Trina Stream's husband isn't he. How's he been doing?"

"Ted and I have worked closely to give Barney a wide range of experiences. He's been in General Branded Marketing, Personnel, Purchasing, Quality & Accuracy, Customer Service, Special Situations, and now, Production," said Tom.

"That's seven positions in nine years," said Rolly. "Why?"

"He's made such an impact in each of his areas that we wanted to round him out with experiences all over First Galaxy. It's always a tough call to move a strong person out of an area," Tom explained.

"There's definitely something special in the Stream family," said Rolly. "Trina's sister works here too, doesn't she?"

"Yes, Gina Stream is my Division Analyst, responsible for budgeting," said Tom. "She's been with First Galaxy about 2 years."

"What level is she?" asked Rolly.

"First Deputy President."

"Promote her to Senior Executive Deputy President and put her in charge of a division," Rolly said. "Make her Director of the Banker Market. We just moved Riichard Shunk to Morale Enhancement so you have an opening. She'll be a great leader in our business areas. Meeting over."

"I'm not sure Gina is ready for this, Rolly. There are a lot more qualified" Tom started.

"Meeting over!" Rolly said sharply and turned his back to Ted and Tom.

Tom and Ted took their leave just as Helen buzzed Rolly on his intercom.

"Rolly, Sid Phlanman from The Breakfast Mission is on the phone. Are you available to speak with him?" Helen asked.

"Sid! What can I do for you?" Rolly said.

"Hello Rolly. I have tremendous news for you. I just got the results of our Community Impact Report for the past year and wanted to share it with you. The Breakfast Mission has provided over 6,000 meals to 500 people, provided clothing to 800 people and job training to 1,000 people. The best news is that 700 of the 1,000 people are now working full time and have become contributing members of our community. One hundred of these people have full-time jobs at First Galaxy, by the way," said Sid.

"Congratulations to you and your organization, Sid. What about the 300 who haven't found jobs yet?"

"The congratulations belong to you, Rolly. It was your personal $8 million endowment that gave us the resources to expand our programs. Your leadership on our Board has also made us focused on results rather than just on dollars. And here is the biggest reason for my call. I called the Delaware Times and the local TV stations and they are going to run a tribute to you and"

"Charity is a private, personal thing," Rolly interrupted. "This is to remain private and anonymous. If you ever publicize my donations, I will cut off all involvement."

"Rolly, I'm sorry. I was just trying to"

"Cut the crap. Now, answer my question. What about the 300 people who haven't found jobs yet?"

"We're working to find them employment. Some of these cases are complex due to medical conditions, criminal records and substance abuse," Sid said.

"You've done some great work, Sid. Put together a regular program rotation to bring more people in and keep them focused on finding work. I'll see you next week at the Board Meeting," and Rolly hung up the phone.

Poor Sid Phlanman. Not only did he just have to deal with Rolly Burnrock, a charter member of the Forbes 400 Ball-busters List, but he lost the office pool again. Sid had an involuntary head tick that caused him to jerk his head up and to the left when he was under stress. Contact with Rolly, whether actual or anticipated, always caused the head ticks. To get some enjoyment out of his ordeal, Sid and his office staff placed bets on the number of head ticks he would have during a phone conversation. Sid was the "house" for the bets. If he had less than 10 ticks in a phone conversation, he won. Anything over 10 and he had to pay everyone $2.00 a piece. Rolly's rant about media publicity tipped the scales and put Sid at 15 head ticks for the call, costing him $12 plus the cost of two extra-strength Tylenols.

"Rolly," Helen buzzed the intercom as soon as the call ended. "Ralph Underock called. He asked to meet with you today on an urgent matter. You're open at 5:30 if you would like to meet with him then."

"OK. Have Ted and Tom attend with me."

Ralph Underock was Director of Special Security Investigations. Keeping a company as large and complex as First Galaxy secure was a major task, and Ralph's military and intelligence background gave him the experience to do a difficult job. Ralph and his staff, most of whom had military and law enforcement backgrounds, had established solid working relationships with police departments where First Galaxy had sites. They shared a common language and common goals, resulting in mutually beneficial relationships.

Chapter 13 – Individual Attention

"Hellooo, this is Riichard," Riich answered his cell phone while driving to his next High School Outreach session. His new role as Director of Morale Enhancement gave him the autonomy he needed so he wasn't tied to his desk all day.

"Hi Riichard. It's James," said James Quill.

"Where are you calling from?" Riichard asked sharply.

"From a pay phone across from school, just like you told me. Don't be angry. I always do what you say," James answered.

"I'm just being careful, for your sake, James. A lot of people would be jealous of our mentoring relationship and its best for you that we keep it as our secret. Stay where you are and I'll be there in about 5 minutes. I got some fresh party supplies for us!"

"Cool. I'm wearing the watch and bracelet you gave me Riichard. Hey, is that the new Justin Timberlake CD you're playing? He's a hottie."

"He sure is. That thing he did with Jeanette Jackson at that football game was gross. Let's stop gabbing, I'll be there in a minute James," and Riich disconnected.

Riich quickly dialed another number.

"Hey stud." the voice on the other end answered.

"Heyyy there. What are you wearing?"

"A pink military uniform, black licorice bra and melon panties. Do you want to eat them?"

"Not only that, I'll supply the whipped cream." Riich said.

"Are you bringing a friend?"

"Yes Nikkie. A high school kid. He's in 12th grade, one year ahead of you. I don't think he's real into girls, so be gentle with him."

"Oooh! I love new students! I'll give you orders while I teach him his lessons. You're bringing the 'teacher's aides' right?" Nikkie squealed.

"What? Don't use that word!"

"What word?"

"Aids. It gives me the creeps."

"Sorry, sexy. How about 'teacher's helpers' instead?"

"Much better. Yeah, I've got enough dust for the FBI to fingerprint the whole county. And I got the Hennessy you like. I'm about to get James, then we'll be over. You're sure your parents are out?" Riich asked.

"They're in Paris. You've asked me a million times already! Tamp yourself down. We're in the clear. Now get moving. My oils are getting cold." Nikkie said and hung up.

Chapter 14 – Paddling Upstream

"First Galaxy, this is Mort Grack."

"This is Gina Stream. I was just told by Mr. Burnrock's office that I have been appointed Director of the Banker Market and that I have been promoted to Senior Executive Deputy President. The org chart I was given says you're the marketing person or was I given incorrect information?"

"Congratulations, Gina. Yes. I am the Marketing Director for the Banker Market. I've been"

"Is your name Mark or Mork?"

"It's Mort."

"Thank you. Why don't you get the staff together in a conference room so I can introduce myself. Hopefully they all showed up for work today. Call my extension when they have gathered, in 5 minutes," and Gina hung up.

"Gina Stream."

"Hello Gina. This is Mort. I have you on the speakerphone. We've gathered in the conference room. If you'd like, we can go around the table and introduce ourselves."

"Let's not waste time. This is Gina Stream. I have been appointed Director of the Banker Market and have been promoted to Senior Executive Deputy President. I have an org chart with your names and titles. My office will be moved to your area in a few days. Will someone please send me the Banker Market goals for this year. I have been told you are very behind on your goals. If someone would put together a report explaining the reasons for the poor performance and send it to me by end of day tomorrow, please."

"Sorry for interrupting, Gina. This is Susie Marshall, a Marketing Coordinator. It's a little hard to hear you. There's some type of loud echo on the phone. It almost sounds like we're hearing everything you say twice."

"I'm talking on my speakerphone. My office is on the floor above you so you're probably hearing an echo. I didn't have time to walk downstairs. So, please get me those reports ASAP. My schedule is very tight the next few weeks. I'm at my sister's Outer Banks house for six days starting day after tomorrow. Then I am on my annual holiday in Europe with Trina. The Annual First Galaxy Executive Management Summit starts right after my holiday. It's in Maui this year and as a Senior Executive Deputy President I will be attending. It's important to get the your performance on track so use the time I am away to develop strategies. My secretary will have the ability to contact me, so if you need to send me any reports, give them to her while I am out. I may need you to put together a presentation for me for the Executive Management Summit and will have my secretary let you know. If there is nothing else, I need to get back to work."

Mort Grack was seething after the phone call. *This is like a bad horror movie, except it's really happening. First I'm stuck with pretty boy Riich and now an ice queen. Who does that bitch think she is talking to us that way? And the passive-aggressive way of talking! I'm through with this place. Two weeks notice, get yourself ready. I'll go work at my father's light bulb factory. It might be boring, but at least I'll have a human being for a boss.*

Chapter 15 – A Shunk In The Armor

Ralph Underock arrived at The Chairman's office at 5:30 sharp. Ted Reilly and Tom Hughman had already arrived.

"What bad news do you have for me today?" Rolly said to Ralph. Ralph was dressed in his trademark gray suit, blue shirt and solid black tie.

"Thank you for seeing me on short notice, Mr. Chairman," Ralph said. Ralph had an understanding with Rolly that if he requested a meeting it was a matter of critical importance.

"Go ahead, Ralph," Rolly said.

"At your request, we've been working with law enforcement to get more information about the incident in Chicago. The issue is more broad-based than just Chicago. Similar incidents have been reported in every city with a First Galaxy site, with the exception of our San Francisco site.

"Local law enforcement in Chicago, Wilmington, New Orleans, San Antonio, and Buffalo have gathered a significant amount of evidence. Since there is a pattern of similar incidents in multiple states, the FBI was brought in by the New Orleans police. Evidence includes photographs, phone intercepts, hospital records, car searches, interviews with several minors and DNA. The evidence clearly indicates the same person was involved in each incident and is a First Galaxy employee." Ralph summarized.

"What are the charges?" Tom asked.

"Cocaine possession, cocaine distribution, statutory rape, sexual abuse of a minor and sodomy of a minor. We also did a thorough background check on the suspect and determined that the information provided when he was hired was largely fabricated. The suspect had the 5th highest travel expenses in the company over the past year despite the fact that his job did not require travel. He covered up the travel by having the expenses charged to his secretary's card so he could approve the expense reports." Ralph finished.

"Who are you saying it is?" Rolly asked.

"Richard Shunk. The evidence is air tight," Ralph answered.

"There must be someone impersonating him. No senior executive of this company could ever do the things you have described," said Rolly.

"Mr. Chairman, at our request the FBI examined for the possibility of an impersonation. They were able to obtain DNA evidence from Mr. Shunk's hair and bodily fluids that were found in the various rental cars, on the kids' clothing and in his company car. There were considerable traces of cocaine in his company car. There were also numerous call intercepts recorded from his company cell phone with drug and sexual related conversations with the kids involved. As is common with this pattern of behavior, the suspect became careless as time went on, believing he was invincible," Ralph answered.

"Is he aware that he is a suspect?" Ted asked.

"We do not believe so, Mr. Reilly," Ralph answered. "Police have issued an APB for him and are searching for him now. His secretary informed us that he disappears for several hours every day and usually returns around 4:30. Police are looking for him at local high schools and are ready if he returns to our site or goes to his residence. Police are confident he will be arrested tonight."

"Thank you Ralph. Keep me informed," Rolly said.

For the first time in 20 years, Rolly felt defeated.

"Tom, Ted, you two are like sons to me. We have been through many good times together and many challenging times. This is the lowest moment of my career. I feel terrible for the kids and the families that were violated. When the time is right I want to speak with the families to express my sorrow. The three of us will personally provide any medical or psychological help the families need."

"Yes, Rolly. It would be a good idea to make a counseling service available to our employees to try to prevent this type of incident from happening again," Ted said.

"There is one more thing related to Shunk. The entire staff in the Bankers Market resigned today. They were very frustrated after reporting to Shunk and indicated that things have gotten even worse with Gina Stream. They expressed a lot of anger that none of them have been promoted in the past two years while senior executives 'get promoted all the time'," Ted said. "I spoke with each of them individually and persuaded all but 2 to stay. Two of them had offers from SuiteBanque for double their salary. I think we need to assess our promotion and recognition programs and improve them."

"Another monster created." Tom said.

"What?" Rolly asked.

"Forget it." Tom said.

"You said 'another monster created.' What did you mean?" Rolly demanded.

"Oh, you did hear me." Tom said. "I meant this is someone brought to First Galaxy through the wave of a hand, with no distinguishing abilities, and spoiled like a king."

"You said 'another.' You think this has happened before?" Rolly barked.

"Not to the level this has reached… no pun intended. We have several people at First Galaxy who were brought to the company in a very expedited manner, who have been fast-tracked into senior level positions without regard to achievement levels or leadership abilities and have become insufferable egoists." Tom said calmly.

"I won't ask you for the names during this conversation, in case you come to your senses and realize the error of your statement. You're saying that you and Ted have failed to perform your leadership development responsibilities. You are supposed to develop these people." Rolly said.

"That sounds reasonable, except how do you develop someone when the Chairman gives them annual promotions and sets their compensation independent of their performance?" Ted said.

"You bastards went along with every decision that has been made! If you did not agree, why didn't you open your mouths? Get out of my office. We have an opening to fill in Morale Enhancement. That position has taken on more importance as a result of today's events."

I guess it's about time we grew the balls to push back on the old man, Tom thought after returning to his office. *He's a business genius, but all the years of iron fist rule have affected his judgment. He's smart enough to realize it, as long as Ted and I push back a little more.*

Ted Reilly had a similar take. *I always knew Alps had balls the size of coconuts. That's what it takes to stand up to the old man. We'll all be better off for it. Maybe we can get things back on the right track. I'll talk to Alps tomorrow and see what else we can do.*

Chapter 16 – Lashin' In Again

Who would be better for the important Morale Enhancement position than someone who was friendly, always said "hello" to employees as he walked past, and showed genuine concern about their daily activities? A Senior Executive whose presence in the hallways or in the meeting room lifted everyone's spirits through sincere friendliness and good spirits. There were so many Senior Executives at First Galaxy with these qualities, but they were already in Very Important Jobs critical to the daily functioning of the company. Most of these Senior Executives *knew* the bank would fall apart without the leadership and executive abilities they brought to work every day. Fortunately, there was a Senior Executive available for the important mission of showing interest in the morale of the employees.

The new Director of Morale Enhancement was very excited about his new position. He knew the importance of appearing friendly and interested towards lower tier employees. He couldn't count the number of times his father had looked up from his bridge game to say 'thankya' to the servant who refreshed his tea cup. Or the many times his father let a servant share some space under the umbrella during a rainstorm, even if that meant a few drops of rain on father's newly cobbled shoes. Most touching of all was the way Mother offered the expired milk to the kitchen staff before it was spilled down the drain.

The Director had the staff assemble in their conference room so he could speak to them. The staff was anxious to meet their new Director. They rarely saw the previous Director and were looking forward to getting someone with a vision for this new department.

"Hwarya. Hwarya. Amma amma amma wut-wuz-it-I-was-gonna-say-to-ya. Amma me name is Barney O'Farkle. I just came here from Production Director, ya know! It was absolutely phenomenal! We were lashin into the producin stuff for all of them affinity groups and the like. I was in on all the meetins about the groups, ya know! I'm over the moon about runnin this here More Enhancin department. I heard you lads have been doing a bang up job and some such. I'm gonna have me secretary schedule some meetins so we can lash right into it and get crackin on all the stuff your doin, ya know. Now do any of you lads have any questions for me?"

"Hello Mr. O'Farkle. I'm Stan Wran and have been here about a month. Do you know when we might work on goals for"

"What? Yes yes yes. Goot goot goot. We'll set up some meetins to lash into the goals."

"Mr. O'Farkle, I'm Mary Padarry. We've heard that we might be moving to"

"What? Amma amma I'll be havin me stuff moved into me new office right off. I'm as excited as the cream filler at the donut shop, ya know. Can one of you lads give the Movers a shout and have me stuff moved? I'm off on holiday for the next two weeks, then I'm amma at the Management Conference Executive Summit meetin in ammmmmm Hawaii. Soon as I get back we're gonna lash into all of the stuff, ya know. I'm off to pick up some chips and butts before the amma car service gives me my lift to the airport. Tap."

Chapter 17 – Cut From The Right Cloth

"Hey Grip! Straighten up the swatches and make sure the suit racks look sharp. Mr. Burnrock will be here in 15 minutes," said Wally Grayson to his son, Daniel "Grip" Grayson.

Wally Grayson was the 3rd-generation owner of Grayson & Son Clothiers, a Wilmington, Delaware icon since the 1930's. One of the few independently owned fine clothing and tailor shops remaining in the United States, Grayson & Son emphasized quality, tradition and service to keep a loyal customer base. One of their best customers was Rolly Burnrock, who started shopping at G&S when First Galaxy moved to Delaware.

Grayson flourished in a competitive business by catering to the ego and clothing needs of his customers. Wally networked with the CEO staff of all the large local companies, including Rolly's, so he could follow the correct protocol for CEO Visits to the store. Wally knew that one slip-up in supporting the Executive Ego would cost him a lot of business. An unpleasant incident 15 years earlier made an indelible mark in Wally's memory:

It was a Tuesday, one of those rare winter days when the mercury hit 60° and stirred one's thoughts of spring. The CEO of a Delaware chemical giant dropped by G&S to get some shirts. Wally recognized him from newspaper articles and greeted him warmly:

"Good morning Mr. Axelrote. I would be happy to assist you."

"Shirts," was the one-word reply.

"Yes sir. We offer the finest tailored shirts and can also create bespoke shirts for you," Wally said, but his words went unheard as Mr. Axelrote brushed past Wally to the glass-shelved display of dress shirts behind the counter.

Starting from the top left-hand corner of the display, Axelrote threw one shirt after another onto the floor, using the motion of a dog digging a hole. As he progressed through the shelves, his face became a deepening shade of red. 15…15 ½…16…16 ½… By the time he reached the 17" collar size, even his hands were red. Wally was afraid Axelrote was going to have a stroke. After about 3 minutes, all the shirts were on the floor. Axelrote turned around, grabbed a handful of ties, and threw them on the floor for good measure.

"How dare you insult me this way!" Axelrote blasted. **"The Goodwill store has a better selection than this dump. You must be selling the shit they couldn't give away! I wear 15 ½ / 34 shirts and you don't have one damn shirt in my size! Change the name of your store to G&S Midget & Fat because you don't carry normal sizes!"** Mr. Axelrote then stormed out of the store, furious that the front door had a pneumatic tube that denied him the pleasure of slamming the door.

Wally, 28 years old at the time, was in shock. His father, Max, was in the back of the store, doubled over in laughter. "What the hell are you laughing at?" Wally yelled.

"Welcome to the clothing business, son. You just took a class in customer relations, presented by Professor Axelrote. Now you'll understand that we are in the ego support business first, and the clothing business second. Let's clean up this mess and see if you learned anything from Professor Axelrote's "class.""

Max Grayson proceeded to tell his son about the Executive Ego and how it demanded that its needs be anticipated and fulfilled. He told Wally about a similar "class" he had taken 20 years earlier when the senior partner of a local law firm tied all the socks in the store together end-to-end, made a big sling shot, and fired every tie within his reach all over the store, all because he could not find a pair of black socks with white micro-dots.

After the incident with "Professor Axelrote" Wally began to network with CEO assistants at every local company. He kept updated Action Plans for every CEO, outlining the protocol for their store visits.

For example, the Action Plan for Axelrote's visits:

- Mr. Axelrote's assistant will provide a 15-Minute Warning before arrival
- All shirts in the display must be size 15 ½ / 34
- All shirts must be facing left-to-right, not front-to-back
- Shirt display must be full; create the appearance that 15 ½ / 34 is the only size G&S carries
- Store temperature must be 67°
- Lighting must be dimmed to ¾ the normal level
- An unopened box of Partagas #8 cigars must be on the far left edge of the front counter, with a clean black crystal ashtray in front of the box. (Axelrote does not smoke).
- Mr. Axelrote must be offered a new white silk handkerchief once he has entered the store and is standing in place.
- No offering or mentioning of food or beverage
- No newspapers or magazines in sight
- Mr. Axelrote wears Hickey-Freeman suits, size 43 exclusively
- Need exactly 18 size 43 Hickeys on the suit rack, all blue solids or stripes.
- Suits must be arranged so that every 3rd suit in the size 43 area is a Hickey, with the in-between suits other, less expensive brands.

Wally arranged to get a "15-Minute Warning" prior to a Rolly's visits, to ensure the store was ready. Wally was training his son Grip in the art of ego support and had recently started to include him in part of the production for Rolly's visits.

G&S was lucky on this particular day, because no customers were in the store during the "15-Minute Warning" period. Part of the protocol for Rolly's visits called for the store to be OPEN, but no customers could be in the store. Upon receiving the 15-Minute Warning, Grayson locked the doors and put up the CLOSED sign until a few minutes before Rolly arrived.

A critical part of the protocol was the Beverage Offering. Rolly had very specific beverage needs and Wally had to be prepared to meet any of them:

Coffee – Costa Rican Daku Estate, ground no more than 10 minutes before consumption, served in a 7.5 oz cup, royal blue color with a gold circle at the cup bottom, 132° temperature, 1.5 oz of cream dispensed from a sterling silver server, and 25 grains of Café DuMonde sugar, stirred 3 times counter-clockwise with a sterling silver spoon. The coffee was to be served on a 6 X 8 inch porcelain tray, silver color, with the cup handle facing to Rolly's left.

Soda – Dr. Brown's Cream Soda was the only carbonated beverage to be offered. No other carbonated beverages were to be on the premises. The soda was to be in a 7.5 oz glass bottle chilled to 44° and poured into an 8.5 oz glass exactly 5" tall, with 4 ice cubes 1x1" in size, in the glass. The soda was to be served on a 5 X 8 inch clear Lucite tray with the ice cubes facing away from Rolly.

Water – Poland Spring water in a 7.5 oz glass bottle, chilled to 46°. The water was to be served with the bottle cap ½ a revolution from removal, next to an 8.5 oz glass exactly 5" tall, with 3 ice cubes, 1x1" in size, in the glass. The water bottle was to be handed to Rolly, with the Poland Spring label facing to Rolly's left. The glass was to be on an 8" X 8" brass tray. Rolly would determine whether to drink from the bottle or ask for the water to be poured into the glass.

"OK, Grip, Two Minute Warning. I'm going to stand by the door and unlock it in 60 seconds. Stand behind me so you can lock it as soon as Mr. Burnrock is inside with his back to the door," Wally said to his son. "I'm going to introduce you to Mr. Burnrock today and let you do the Beverage Offering. You've seen it plenty of times and I know you can handle it. Get ready, I see him coming."

"Good afternoon, Mr. Burnrock. It is a pleasure to welcome you," Wally said as Rolly arrived.

"What kind of moth-infested crap do you have today?" Rolly said.

"We have the summer custom offerings from Oxxford, if you would like to see them," Wally said. Rolly wore Oxxford Suits exclusively.

"Well, where are they?" Rolly said.

"I will show them to you right away. May I offer you a beverage?" Wally offered.

"What have you got?" Rolly replied. This was part of the protocol: the Beverage Offer, followed by the "what have you got" test.

"We have Costa Rican Daku Estate coffee, Dr. Brown Cream Soda and Poland Spring Water," said Wally.

"Is that all you have?" Rolly said.

"Yes, Mr. Burnrock." Wally replied per the script.

"I will have coffee."

"Thank you, sir. My son Grip will bring it right out to you. With your permission, I would like to introduce him to you. He is on break from college and is helping me for the summer," Wally said.

Grip arrived with the coffee and put on a masterful performance. "Hello Mr. Burnrock. I am Grip Grayson. I would like to present this cup of Costa Rican Daku Estate coffee, brewed 4 minutes ago from just-ground beans. The coffee has 1.5 oz of cream, 25 grains of Café DuMonde sugar and was stirred 3 times counter-clockwise. It will be my pleasure to wait for your approval of the coffee."

Rolly was instantly impressed with Grip. Grip had the qualities Rolly liked: About 5'3" tall, thin in a non-athletic way, thick hair parted at the side, winning smile, perfect posture, solid eye contact and confident voice.

"Where did you get the name Grip?" Rolly asked.

"I got it in 7th grade after competing in the school-wide Pull-Up contest," Grip replied.

"Does that mean you won?" Rolly asked.

"I finished in 2nd place."

"What year are you in college, Grip?"

"I'm in my final year for my MBA in Marketing from University of Delaware. I have a B.A. in Marketing from Notre Damius University, sir."

"Dammit Wally! Why didn't you tell me your son went to Notre Damius? That's where I went. When do you graduate Grip?"

"December, sir."

"I want you at First Galaxy. You will get a phone call from one of my assistants the last week of November. You'll start the day after graduation. Enough horse shit, Wally. Show me some suits."

That was 4 years ago. Daniel "Grip" Grayson was now 28 and consumed with ambition. After only 4 years with First Galaxy, Grip had been promoted three times and was Executive Deputy President responsible for the Careers & Degrees Market. The Careers & Degrees (C&D) market housed First Galaxy's most prestigious affinity relationships, including George Kreble's SACP, plus the largest lawyer, medical and educator associations in the U.S.

Grip had been transferred to C&D three months earlier, following two years as head of the Quality & Accuracy division. Grip contributed several innovations during his tenure in Q&A. He was most proud of the *Daily Digest*, the company's intranet site. The site enabled employees to receive company updates online every day, saving millions of dollars in paper, printing and delivery costs. Grip also developed the *Daily Executive Action Digest*, a 2-page paper version of the online site, delivered to all Senior Executives with **PUBLISHED BY GRIP GRAYSON, EXECUTIVE DEPUTY PRESIDENT** printed boldly at the top. Grip was unaware that most of the report's recipients referred to it by its initials, "DEAD," and liked to say they "dropped DEAD" when they tossed it in the trash can upon arrival.

One of Grip's biggest innovations was the source of his biggest embarrassment. He created an employee suggestion program to tap ideas for improving products, services and operations. Grip developed the program all by himself and knew it had to have an action-oriented name. He chose the name *Find...Understand...Contribute* to encourage employees to keep their eyes open for anything that would help First Galaxy better serve customers. Grip was so excited that he ordered 10,000 laminated cards describing the program. The day after sending the order for the cards to the Reproduction Center he got a call from the Senior Lamination Officer.

"This is Grip Grayson."

"Hello Mr. Grayson. This is Dick Stemlem in the Reproduction Center. I'm calling about your FUC Program."

"My *what* program? What are you talking about?"

"Mr. Grayson, we were getting ready to type-set your job and noticed that you wanted the first letters in *Find... Understand... Contribute* in bold. The letters F, U, and C really stand out and will possibly be pronounced as FUC."

"Wait a minute....SHIT!! You're right," Grip said, instantly panicked because he had sent prototypes to Tom and Ted earlier in the day. "Hold on a minute. I had written down some other names and just need to find my list..... OK. Use this one: *Start Noticing Opportunity Today.*"

"Let's see. If we go with the same type-set style, that will be the SNOT program," Dick said, doing his best not to laugh. *This guy is more uptight than Al Gore at a hip-hop concert.*

"DAMMIT! Use this one: *Study... Learn... Identify... Contribute.* What do those initials spell?" Grip asked.

I'm not dealing with a Mensa club member here, Dick thought. "That would be SLIC, Mr. Grayson."

"Go with that. Anything else?" Grip said.

"That's it. We should have the cards to you tomorrow, Mr. Grayson. Thank you," Dick said. *Why am I thanking him? I just saved the brainless moron's job.*

Just as Grip got off the phone with Dick Stemlem, Ted Reilly called.

"Hello Ted. This is Grip."

"Hey Grip. I'm here with Tom Hughman and we want to FUC," Ted said, followed by explosive laughter.

"Excuse me, sir?" Grip replied, wondering what Ted was talking about.

"We're looking at the prototype for your employee suggestion program and we'd like to FUC. I bet a lot of our employees will want to FUC. Sounds like you got a real winner here, Grip. Let's see... if I submit an idea that gets implemented, I get $75 and a plaque that says "I FUC'd today. And if someone tries to horn in on my idea, I can tell them to go FUC themselves." Ted said.

"I'm sorry Ted and Tom. I just got off the phone with the Reproduction Center and told them to cancel the job. I caught the mistake before anything was printed or type-set. I've come up with a different name, *Study... Learn... Identify... Contribute.* Same program details."

"OK Grip. We'll keep these prototypes as souvenirs," Ted hung up, still laughing.

Grip regretted that he didn't have any of his staff work on the program. That left him with no one else to blame for the biggest "FUC up" of his career.

Chapter 18 – Billionaire Needs More Money

"Sammy Shifster is on the phone for you, Ted."

"Thanks, June. I'll pick up in a minute," Ted Reilly responded to his assistant. *Let's see if Sammy is calling with a follow-up about the swiss cheese information security at SPS,* Ted thought, dreading yet another conversation with Shifster.

"Sammy. How's the weather in Daytona Beach? What's up?" Ted said.

"OK my lawyers updated all the non-compete agreements to remain in force for 24 months after getting fired.... I mean, after employees leave SPS. Locks have been put on all the office doors and a clean-desk policy is in place. The latest C&D account plans are too low and the Retailer Market isn't putting on any accounts at all. This also is a good time to extend the contract between SPS and First Galaxy so I'll send one down for your signature. I think you mean Palm Beach, not Daytona. What else?" Sammy finished. He liked to multi-task his phone conversations, to keep the other party off guard and to give himself a lot of "outs" to change the subject.

"I forgot to tell you that we've moved Barney O'Farkle to our new Morale Enhancement department. I'm starting to have second thoughts about the move and, just thinking out loud, wonder if I should leave him as Production Director," Ted said. *Shifty must be under some stress. I can hear the crinkling of his bag of chips. He can hardly talk, his mouth is so full of chips. Time to break out the large size Brioni's.* "From what Barney has told me, you two have really bonded.

Hold on and I'll get Barney on this call and you two can discuss the account plans and all the other stuff."

"Wait! Slow down a minute. I'm the last one to tell you what to do with your organizational structure, Ted, but that morals and ethical stuff is important. Believe me, I know because I spend a lot of time on that stuff with my staff. If you've got a good man like Barney in that role, that's very important for the bank," Sammy said.

"You're right Sammy. Barney is a good man. That's why I'm moving him back to Production. He'll be your day-to-day contact about the issues you raised…. the account plans and contract renewal. Those are important items and Barney is just the guy to lash into it and set up some meetins," Ted replied.

"You know what might be even better, Ted? Let's table the account plan and contact extension discussions. We can get to that some other time, after Barney is fully settled in his new department and you've had time to find someone to fill his shoes in Production."

"If that's what you want, Sammy. Go easy on the chips." and Ted hung up.

What's gotten into him? Sammy thought. *The last few weeks he's developed a real negative attitude. I'll take some of the load off him by going through Tom on these issues.* Sammy had to put his thoughts on hold because he broke into a coughing fit from all the nacho chip dust he was inhaling. His face, hands, shirt and phones were covered with orange nacho smears. Sammy had to use two hands to hang the phone up because the receiver was stuck to his hand from the build-up of wet nacho residue.

Chapter 19 – I Like Leather Chairs

"Damn, James. You dived into Nikkie like a man having his last meal." Riich said to James Quill as they drove back from their party.

"She was incredible, Riichard! You were too. Can we party with her again?"

Riich dropped James Quill at the shopping center across from his high school. Riich looked at himself in the rear-view mirror with pride. *Who else devotes so much time and effort to young people?*

Riich checked his watch and saw it was only 4:15. He decided to run into the office before going to his next important meeting.

As he passed the high school on the way to I-95, he saw several police cars by the school entrance. *Must be those gangsta kids causing trouble again,* Riich thought. The police must have been finishing up, because several of them pulled onto the road behind Riich's car. *At least I won't have to worry about getting carjacked. A well-dressed white executive in a Mercedes S Class car is a real target in this neighborhood. It's too bad James can't see this; I could tell him I have a police escort because I'm a Senior Executive at a Major Financial Institution! Oh, cool; the cars are putting their strobe lights on and one of them is pulling in front of me. They're giving me an escort!! This must be part of the new Senior Executive Protection Plan at First Galaxy. I wonder if we'll be able to run some red lights!*

Riich's thoughts were interrupted by the piercing sound of police sirens as the unit in front of him came to a stop and the other cars boxed him in. One of the Officers walked up to his car. *This must be a dress-rehearsal,* Riich thought.

"Are you Richard Shunk?" the first officer asked.

"Hellooo. How ARE you? Yes, I am Riichard Shunk."

"Please step out of the car, Mr. Shunk," the Officer said as three Officers surrounded the car.

"What is going on, Officer?" Riich demanded.

"Please step out of the car now," the Officer said while opening the car door.

Riich stepped out, brushing a white powdery substance off his pants. "Can you hand me my cashmere overcoat from the backseat. It's cold outside." Riich said to the Officer.

"Mr. Shunk, you are under arrest for cocaine possession, cocaine distribution, statutory rape, and kidnapping. The crimes you are accused of crossed state lines, making them federal offenses. Arrest warrants have been issued in Delaware, Louisiana and Michigan. We are impounding your vehicle as evidence and will transport you to the County Detention Center for processing and questioning. After that you will appear before a judge to enter your plea. If you want your coat, get it yourself." The Officer explained while placing handcuffs on Riich.

"No no no," Riich whined. "I thought you were protecting me. I didn't do any of the things you just said. Let me go Officer. How dare you treat a Senior Executive like this! You are making a big mistake!"

"Officer Miranda here will read you your rights."

Riich was taken to the Wilmington police station a few blocks from First Galaxy headquarters. After processing, he was brought to an interrogation room. The room smelled like a combination of orange peels, brussel sprouts and piss. They put him in a wooden chair at the side of a square metal table. There was a tape recorder in the middle of the table.

This is gross! Riich thought. *This floor probably hasn't been cleaned in years. I'm going to have to tell them that my feet are allergic to linoleum and I can't stay in this room. Don't they have special rooms for Senior Executives, with nice carpeting and paneling on the walls? They don't even have a PC or a speaker phone in here. It's probably taking them a long time to come in here because they're too embarrassed to admit they brought me in by mistake.*

After about 20 minutes, two officers entered the room.

"Mr. Shunk, I am Detective Breelan and this is Detective Gulanda. We're going to ask you some questions and then take you to the courthouse for arraignment. Do you understand?"

"Helloo Detectives. How ARE you? It's a little chilly in this room and this chair is very uncomfortable. I'm used to leather chairs and prefer a room temperature of 69°. Can one of you run out and get me some tea? I take it with 1 ounce of skim milk and ½ packet of raw sugar. I prefer gourmet tea, but if all you have is store brand, bring that. In a glass please, not styrofoam."

"Shut up asshole. Enjoy this room because it'll be the most comfortable place you're going to be for a long time. Let me give you the ground rules. In a few minutes, I will turn the recorder on and ask you a series of questions. It is in your best interest to answer the questions honestly and directly. Should you have any memory lapses or give an answer that does not match up with the evidence against you, I will pause the tape and Detective Gulanda will administer some memory stimulation and truth encouragement procedures. Let's get started."

"Excuse mee. I want my lawyer," Riich said.

"Absolutely, Mr. Shunk. There is a lawyer in the waiting area for you. His name is Thom Pathic and he said he is from MLBA," Breelan said as he looked at his notes.

"MLBA…. That must be the major league baseball association. I brought them to First Galaxy and have season tickets for every team in the league. They really love me and must have sent one of their top lawyers to help me. I wonder how they heard about this so fast." Riich said.

"If you want to stop this session to talk with a lawyer, Detective Gulanda and I will go ahead and consult with you right now on the benefits of obtaining legal counsel," Detective Breelan said as he and Gulanda rolled their sleeves up. Gulanda wrapped a towel around a thick, shiny night stick. He walked behind Riich and slammed him across the back with the stick.

"Let me help you back into this non-leather chair, Mr. Shunk," Detective Breelan said as he raised Riich up and bounced him back into the chair.

"Now, you want your lawyer, or should I start the tape recorder?" Detective Breelan asked.

"Ask your questions, but I'm going to file a complaint against"

Riich was interrupted by the towel whipping against the back of his head.

"Sorry. What did you say?" Detective Breelan asked.

"Go ahead," Riich gasped.

"Do you know a James Quill?"

"Yes. I met him as part of the high school outreach I do."

"Have you given cocaine to James Quill?"

"James and I are good friends. We do Outreach together. I've helped a lot of kids that way."

"What about Nicole Sugarus? Do you know her?"

"The name sounds familiar. She must be another kid I've mentored."

"Were you in New Orleans, Louisiana from May 28-31 this year?"

"Yes. I was there to address a critical attendance issue at my company where I am a Senior Executive."

"A car matching the one you rented in New Orleans was parked across the street from New Orleans High School during the dates you were in town. Did you meet a Christopher Jeffish and Susie Looplop, give them cocaine and engage in sex acts with them?"

"You can ask my secretary Victoria. She was there. I told her I was going to do Outreach while we were there. That's how I met Chris and Susie."

Detective Breelan pushed the pause button on the tape recorder.

"Let me give you an 'Executive Summary' of the case against you," Detective Breelan said, and explained the DNA, bodily fluid, drug residue, hospital records, photographic and sworn evidence police and FBI agents had gathered in Delaware, Louisiana and Michigan.

"We have air-tight evidence against you. You have two alternatives: Deny the charges and face extradition hearings and trials in three states, with maximum sentences totaling four life terms, or you can plead guilty today and get 35 years with no parole," Detective Breelan said.

"I did not do anything wrong," Riich said in his trademark whine. "When did it become a crime to show friendship to young people? I can't get a fair trial against all this made-up evidence. Ever since the right-wing took over this country, all of our freedoms have been taken away. We're living in a fascist state. Rather than be in a police state that makes up evidence against me, I will take the 35 years. If that means I have to say I did the things you mentioned, it's better than letting you put on a Stalinist show trial to further your right-wing fascist goals," Riich said.

"Stalin was a Marxist, Mr. Shunk, not right wing, but let's not argue politics. I'm going to turn the tape recorder on. I want you to state in detail the dates, locations, people and acts you engaged in. If you leave anything out, I'll pause the tape and administer a refresher to you. Then you will go before the judge." Detective Breelan said.

"Go ahead Generalissimo," Riich said, ducking too late to miss another back slam from Detective Gulanda.

After the court hearing, Riich asked to make a phone call.

"Detective, I would like to make the phone call I am entitled to."

"Use the pay phone outside the interrogation room."

Riich decided to call his wife to let her know he would not be home for a while.

"Hi sweetie, it's Richard. I have some very exciting news. I've been selected to be on a brand new reality TV show called 'Who Wants To Be A Criminal.' I saw an ad in the paper a few months ago asking for volunteers and decided to go for it. In order to qualify, I had to do a few little things like jay-walk and shoplift. Anyway, the producers love me and have become some of my best friends and I just got called tonight saying they want me on the show. I had to do a few more little things so they could film me "going through the system" so I could end up in jail for the show. I'm in the jailhouse right now! It's really exciting here. The people here love me. To keep it real, even the police and the judge think I committed real crimes. The only bad thing about this is I won't be able to come home until the series is over. The producers think the show is going to be a big hit so it could be a real long time before I get out. They're going to film a full season of shows before it goes on the air, so it probably won't even be on until next year. I think they said you can visit in a few weeks but I need to find out. The phone is starting to beep. I guess that means I need to get off. Love you and the kids. Byyeeeee."

Chapter 20 – Out And About

"YES!!!!"

Debbie Shunk screamed so loud she almost gave her friend a stroke.

"What is it?" Bob asked, checking to see if his heart was still inside his chest.

" 'IT' is the call I've been waiting to get for 2 years!" Debbie exclaimed. "My sociopath perverted pile of shit husband was finally caught in his web of lies. The police just arrested him for something. He didn't say what it was, just made up some bull shit about spending time in jail for some reality TV show. He doesn't know I hired a private investigator years ago and know all about his perverted activities.

"I've just started the payback. I sent a lawyer from MLBA, the *Men Loving Bi Association* to be his lawyer. I picked a lawyer with a loser name like Thom Limpdick or something. Richard is such a brainless moron he'll probably think the lawyer is from Major League Baseball. Wait till the article hits the paper about who MLBA really is! Enough about Richard. Pour me some more wine," Debbie commanded.

At the age of 36, Debbie Elizabeth Bolyan Laughlin Shunk's life was a far cry from the picture-book journey she dreamed about as a child. Debbie grew up in Milford, Delaware, a rural town of simplicity and honesty. She had two loving parents, two brothers and one sister. As the second youngest of four children, Debbie learned to appreciate the things she had. Her parents instilled the values of honesty, trust, hard work and appreciation into her from a young age.

Debbie grew to be a strikingly beautiful young lady and became head cheerleader at Milford Vocational High School starting in the 10th grade. Through her participation in the cheerleaders, she met and fell in love with one of the clarinetists in the marching band. Debbie loved the routines the cheerleaders performed with the band and liked the esprit de corps of the group. She got to know Dan Laughlin, the first-chair clarinetist in the band, during their first semester as freshmen. Even though the clarinets were drowned out by the brass instruments, Debbie admired Dan's spirit and the way he played. As their friendship developed, she enjoyed the hours they would spend listening to Pete Fountain records.

Debbie and Dan's friendship grew into love as they moved into their junior year in high school. Both were from families of modest means and did not plan to attend college. After graduation, Dan parlayed his love of music into a job at the *Fine Tunes Music Store* in Dover, the capital of Delaware. He sold instruments, did some instrument repairs and taught lessons. This was Dan's dream job: getting paid to do what he enjoyed. Two nights a week, Dan played with a Dixieland band at a small lounge in Rehoboth Beach, to earn extra money and to fulfill his fantasy of pretending he was Pete Fountain.

Debbie went to work for *Winnie's Wall of Wine and Sausage*, the largest wine and gourmet sausage merchant in Milford. Winnie's was owned by Winthrope Sweethash, the father of one of Debbie's high school friends. Through her work as a cashier, inventory assistant and event planner at Winnie's, Debbie developed a strong interest in wine and a revulsion for sausage.

Debbie and Dan married two months after high school graduation. They were deeply in love and believed fate had brought them together. Debbie became pregnant shortly after they got married and was a mother at 19 years of age. A few months after their first child Anna was born, Debbie became pregnant again. At the age of 20, Debbie and Dan had each other and two children, Anna and Frank.

The Laughlin's lived in happiness and enjoyed their home and professional lives. Dan's clarinet talent developed to the point where he was playing with jazz bands three nights a week. He especially liked Mardi Gras time in mid-February. Mardi Gras gave his band a chance to highlight the New Orleans jazz they loved and add some Second Line marching to their performances.

Dan was really excited about the Mardi Gras 2000 celebration. As the first Mardi Gras of the new century, he felt an extra jolt of electricity in the crowd. The crowd at *Bourbon Street Beach* was wall-to-wall on Mardi Gras night, February 2000. People and alcohol were everywhere. The floor was slick with sweat, grease and spilled drinks. *Bourbon Street Beach* had recently installed a new stage that sat 3 feet above the floor. A varnished staircase led from the stage to the floor.

As the band kicked out 'Oh Didn't He Ramble', a traditional New Orleans second line song, Dan led the way off the stage and down the stairs. The stairs were like an ice-covered road from all the spilled drinks and greasy food. Dan placed his foot on the first step, concentrating on his solo and not on the stairs. He slipped on the first step, tripped over a spectator and landed face down with his clarinet still in his mouth. The force of the fall pushed his clarinet through his head like a sword. Dan died instantly.

After the pain and shock from Dan's passing began to ease, Debbie had to plan her family's future. She was 31 years old, with a 12 year old daughter and 11 year old son. Dan's life insurance and the savings they had built from his jazz playing provided a modest level of financial security. Debbie's interest in wine and desire to expose her children to a more active lifestyle led her to move to the Wilmington area in late 2000.

There were several top quality wine merchants in Wilmington. Debbie took a position at a small, family owned store, *Grapes On The Vine*. Debbie was a jack-of-all-trades, dispensing advice, managing the inventory and ringing up sales. Debbie enjoyed the breadth and depth of the store's wine selection and the opportunity to interact with the upscale customers in the Wilmington area. Unlike Milford, customers in Wilmington did not hesitate to spend $100's of dollars on a bottle of wine or $1,000's on cases of wine. The elevated scope and pace of her responsibilities helped ease the pain of Dan's passing.

Every January, Rolly Burnrock conducted "Balance" sessions with a random selection of his senior executives. Rolly used the sessions to ensure his executives lead wholesome lives outside of First Galaxy and properly balanced their personal and professional responsibilities.

In January 2001, Rolly was scheduled to meet with Riichard Shunk, who had not been selected for a Balance session since 1994. While reviewing Riichard's file, Rolly was impressed by the 25 positions Riich had occupied at First Galaxy, interpreting the high level of movement as evidence of a well-rounded career. The one area of Riich's record with blank space was family. Rolly was surprised that a 46 year old male making good money was not married.

"Hellooo. How ARE you?" Riich said to Rolly's secretary as he entered the outer suite to Rolly's offices, head held high, winning smile on his face.

"May I help you?" Helen asked.

"I'm here for my 2:00 with Rolly, Helen. I'm Riichard Shunk, Executive Deputy President. I've been with First Galaxy since 1990 and was hired directly by Rolly and have had 25"

"Yes, Mr. Shunk. Please be seated. Mr. Burnrock will be ready for you in a few minutes."

"Please go into Mr. Burnrock's conference room, Mr. Shunk," Helen said a few minutes later. Rolly made every visitor wait at least 10 minutes.

"Richard Shunk. What brings you here today?" Rolly said when he entered the conference room.

"Helloo Rolly. How ARE you. I'm here for our annual Balance session. I've learned so much from you from these sessions and they have really helped me grow and succeed as a senior executive here at First Galaxy," Riich gushed with his winning smile, laser eye contact and perfect posture.

"Annual Balance session? We haven't met since 1994 according to my records. Are you saying I have bad information?" Rolly demanded.

"I remember that 1994 session so well. I think of your Special Monthly Management Meetings as part of these sessions in my mind since I value the opportunity to hear your thoughts so much that it"

"The two sessions are completely different. You must not be very bright if you can't tell the difference," Rolly said. "I've looked at your file, the one showing our last 'annual' meeting was in 1994. It looks like your career is moving along well and that you have been performing at an exceptional level. Unless that part of the file is wrong as well. What is going on in your life outside First Galaxy? A fine young man like yourself should be married and have children by now. Are you working so hard that you don't have time for a social life?"

"Guilty as charged, Rolly. The days here just fly by. I'm in at 7 and by the time I turn around, it's 8 or 9 at night. I guess I've neglected my social life so I could devote my energies to First Galaxy. I've made so many good friends here that this seems like family to me." Riich said.

"What about weekends?" Rolly asked.

"I've been spending time at various housing projects in the area helping to rebuild run-down units. While I'm there a lot of the residents ask me for advice on how to find a job and how to manage their money. It's really gratifying to see the happy looks on their faces when I'm there. They all love me. When I'm not at the housing projects, I either take work home or come in."

"That's quite a story. I'll ask Breeze Penner to contact you to get the names of the housing projects so First Galaxy can donate some building materials and other things they need."

"That's very generous of you Rolly. I've asked them about it and they told me they prefer to be self-sufficient and do not want any outside donations," Riich replied, a hint of perspiration forming on his forehead.

"I'll have him contact you anyway. First Galaxy is a family-oriented company. Every Senior Executive Deputy President here is happily married. You may not reach your potential here without the proper balance in your life," Rolly said as he stood up and left the conference room, signifying the meeting was over.

Wow. He really likes me! Riich thought. He just about came out and said he wants to promote me to Senior Executive Deputy President. If I have to get married to get promoted, so be it.

Shortly after his Balance session, Riich pursued women as if it were another Important Project.

Since joining *Grapes On The Vine*, Debbie had observed an energetic, youthful-looking customer who visited the store a few times each week. He always had a smile on his face and seemed to be in a hurry to get some place. He had a unique way of saying "hello," making it sound like there were three syllables. The customer asked her to show him specific wines from time to time, but never engaged in conversation. He often looked at his watch as she showed him the wine.

Riich stopped at *Grapes On The Vine* a few days after his talk with Rolly. He noticed an attractive female clerk at the store and was fairly certain she had retrieved wine for him on previous visits. He decided to talk with her as part of his new "project."

"Hellooo. How ARE you. You're looking very lovely today. My name is Richard. I've seen you here many times but I've been so busy going to important social events or hosting important receptions at my residence, that I did not have time to introduce myself. What is your name?" Riich asked, extending a firm hand and flashing his winning smile.

"Hi. I'm Debbie. I've seen you here a lot. You seem to know a lot about wine."

"I'm a Senior Executive for a very large bank and I'm always being invited to dinner with very good friends and to important receptions so I have an ongoing need for wine. Wine Spectacular magazine asked me to write an article about wine selection strategies because I am one of their best subscribers. As soon as I find some time in my busy schedule, I'll try to respond to their request."

"That's interesting." Debbie said, wondering how one became a 'best subscriber' to a magazine.

"I'm on my way to one of my best friends' mansion. They invited me to dinner and asked me to select the wine, since I always pick just the right wine. I was thinking of the Opus Grande Imperial Pinot Noir, 1978 vintage."

"I believe we have it available," Debbie said. "If you would like to follow me, I will locate it for you."

"That's a very pretty dress you're wearing. Is it silk?"

"Thank you. Here it is. We have three bottles available," Debbie said upon finding the wine. "We also have the Opus Platinum 1976 vintage that our customers rave about. They say it has incredible depth and a beautiful finish. Wine Spectacular gave it a 92 rating."

"Yes. I am familiar with it. I've had it many times at important social events I've attended. I was guest speaker at a high level banking conference last year and they gave me a bottle as a gift in addition to my honorarium. Go ahead and give me one bottle of the Opus Platinum and two bottles of the Grande Imperial," Riich replied.

"Excellent choice, Richard. I'm glad we finally had the chance to talk. Let's go up front and I'll ring you up. The total is $428."

"Here you go," Riich said, handing Debbie his First Galaxy Business Credit Card. *This is definitely a business expense since I'm here at Rolly's request.*

"Thank you Richard. I hope to see you again soon," Debbie said.

"As soon as I clear some time in my busy schedule, I'd like to take you to dinner and talk about wine. I will have my secretary look at my schedule and see if she can find an availability. Maybe we could even attend one of the important social events that I am constantly invited to, if that doesn't interfere with your work schedule. Gotta run, Debra. Thankkkssssss," and Riich was out the door as the "ssssssss" hung in the air.

She adores me! How would a wine clerk ever get to meet an important Senior Executive like me if I did not make the effort to speak to her. Riich replayed the conversation in his mind as he went home to use the wine on his latest Outreach friend. He thought about serving the wine in empty soda cans, like he had heard about on the news recently, but decided that might be tacky.

After a few weeks of friendly in-store banter and occasional phone conversations, Riich took Debbie to dinner at one of his favorite French restaurants. It was an intimate bistro in Kennett Square where Riich often ate. He was good friends with the maitre de, Gordon Mahlow.

"Good evening Mr. Shunk. Welcome back to L' Fruitage. We have your regular table ready for you," Gordon said.

"Hellooo Gordon. How ARE you? I would like you to meet my friend Debra. Debra, this is Gordon Mahlow, one of my best friends. I practically helped open this restaurant," Riich said.

"Yes. Riichard is one of our most special customers," Gordon gushed in return.

After they were seated in a quiet corner, Riich said, "Have you ever been to a place this nice Debra?"

"This is a beautiful restaurant Richard. Did Gordon call you "Reach-ard?"

"Gordon is always embellishing his French accent. That's probably why it sounded like that. Since this is all probably new to you, I can order for you. Of course you know I can select the right wine," Riich giggled.

Over the course of the evening, Riich told Debbie his version of his life story: childhood spent in New York, star basketball and baseball player in high school, graduated 2nd in his class, college at SUNY, delivered the Student's Speech at graduation and has been asked to speak at every graduation since because his speech received the best ovation ever. Selected by Rolly Burnrock to be a senior executive at First Galaxy right after graduation from SUNY. He and Rolly had been great friends ever since. He sometimes could not believe how much money he made at First Galaxy, but then again $300,000 a year plus bonus was not *that* much when one considered all the things he did for the bank.

When Riich got around to asking Debbie about herself, she told Riich about her marriage to Dan, their wonderful children, and his tragic death.

"Oh my gosh. That is terrible. I am so sorry for you and your children," Riich said after reaching to hold Debbie's hands.

"What about you Richard? How come a handsome, successful man like you hasn't been snatched up?" Debbie asked.

"Well… its….. its hard to talk about," Riich said, covering his face with his hands.

"Please tell me. It's ok," Debbie said.

"You're the first person I've ever told this to. I feel comfortable with you. You're a sweet lady," Riich said, using a tissue to dry his eyes and nose.

"I always dreamed about getting married and having children. But my dreams were shattered my senior year in high school. I was the starting 3rd baseman for the varsity baseball team. I had been voted MVP in my sophomore and junior years and was great friends with everyone on the team. Even the players on the other teams loved me.

"One day we were playing our division rival. I accidentally arrived late because I think I was tutoring a 10th grader and lost track of time. I was in such a rush to take the field that I forgot to put on my protective cup. In the 4th inning, my team was in the field and there were men on 1st and 2nd base. The batter hit the hardest line drive I have ever seen. It came right at me on 3rd base. Before I could react, the ball hit me in my private parts. I doubled over in pain just as the runner was approaching 3rd base. He slid head first, but he started his slide too late and he speared me in my private parts. That's one reason I can't listen to Brittney Spears music because her last name is a reminder of what happened to me that day. I was in such pain that I blacked out for awhile.

"I was in the hospital for 2 weeks recovering. The nurses said they had never seen anyone recover so quickly from such a serious injury and that it must have been because I was in such great shape. Anyway, the worst day of my life was when the doctor came in and gave me the news that shattered my dreams," and Riich buried his head in his hands and made crying sounds.

Debbie came over to his side of the table to comfort Riich. "What a terrible thing you went through. It took a lot of courage for you to share this with me. What did the doctor say to you?" Debbie asked.

After wiping his eyes and blowing his nose, Riich continued. He was glad he had rubbed black pepper on his hands before picking Debbie up.

"He told me…. He said I had permanent damage to my ability to…. This is just so embarrassing… He said I would not be able to have children," Riich again buried his face in his hands, this time putting his face in the handkerchief he had sprinkled with pepper.

"That's why I haven't dated or tried to get married," Riich said. "I was afraid of what would happen when my date found out. It's just that you are so sweet and so beautiful that I just had to take the chance with you. If you don't want to see me anymore, I'll understand."

"No no no," Debbie said soothingly. "Of course I'd like to see you. I'm so sorry for the pain you've been carrying. Since we're being honest with each other, I should tell you something as well."

"Go ahead, Debra. Honesty is very important in a relationship. Its one of my most important values and one of my best qualities."

"Well, I've told you how close Dan and I were. He was my soul mate. I still remember the first time I saw him. We both believed we were made for each other. Its been a little over a year since he died and the pain has only gone down a little bit. I'd like to have a relationship again, but I don't want to be intimate until I feel ready. Also, I don't want to have more children because I want to focus my love and attention on Anna and Frank," Debbie said.

"I understand. It's almost as if fate brought us together as well. We can be like roommates or best friends if that's what you want to do… until you feel ready." Riich giggled, giddy that things were going so well.

"It looks like our food is coming. Let's talk about something less intense," Debbie said.

Riich invited Debbie over to his house after dinner. He explained how the whole house, all 6,000 square feet of it, had been decorated by one of his best friends, Topp Tithelly, and how they had picked out the furniture in North Carolina and got one of the best deals ever. Riich was especially proud of his art collection and showed Debbie his original Maplethorpe and his rare Warhol print.

"The Maplethorpe is interesting," Debbie said. It looks like two people embracing, but I can't tell if they're male or female. And what is the purpose of the jar of lemonade next to them?"

Riich and Debbie continued to spend a lot of time together. He spared no (company) expense showing her how much he cared. They took trips to the Napa Valley for wine seminars, traveled to New York for Broadway shows and even flew to Paris on the spur of the moment. There was occasional kissing and hugging, but Riich respected Debbie's wishes and did not go further.

Riich put all expenses related to Debbie on his First Galaxy Business Credit Card, since he was on a special project for Rolly. After a few months of high expenses, Riich's manager wondered why he was spending over $5,000 a month on travel and entertainment when his job never took him farther than his desk. One morning, Riich's boss called to discuss the expenses.

"Amma amma top of the day to ya laddie. How about if you skip over to me office so we can have a meetin about the amma amma amma wut-wuz-it-again the ummmm budget."

In early 2001, Riich was in job #25, in the Quality & Accuracy department. His boss, Barney O'Farkle, was in job #4, Director of Q&A. Barney was the perfect boss for Riich: as long as Riich sent him a regular stream of voluminous reports Barney was happy.

"Hwarya. You've been busier than a one-armed paper hanger haven't ya? Its one of the few times I get to see your face in person, ya know? Let's lash into some of these amma amma budget reports, ya know!" Barney said as he lit a cigarette.

"Helloooo. How ARE you? Barney, how come you're smoking a cigarette in your office? Isn't that against company policy?" Riich asked.

"What? Somebody broke a policy? Give Audit a shout and have them lash right into it. We can't be havin none of that kind of thing and such around here, ya know! Before I met Trina and I was workin at the fast food pub, I caught a lad stealin chips right out of the freezer. I gave Security a shout and had them lash right into it. They circled the fences and brought the scoundrel to justice. They had me sit in on some of the meetins about it and I signed some of the reports. I used to love deep fryin them fishes and dippin them in the cheese, butter and mayo, ya know! Did ya say something about cigarettes?"

"Yes. I've never seen you smoke in the office before. Aren't you concerned about second-hand smoke?" Riich asked.

"What? Second-hand smoke? Ya mean when a lad is smokin two butts at a time, one in his first hand and one in his second hand, ya know! With all the pressure in me job I need to have me a butt every now and again, ya know? Do ya ever get the urge to ammmm suck on a butt yourself?" Barney asked.

"Excuse me? Oh, cigarettes. No, I've never smoked. I'm very careful about what goes in my body. What did you want to meet about?" Riich said to change the subject.

"What? Tom Hughman's budget assistant, me sister-in-law Gina, gave me a shout yesterday about our Travel and Information amma amma Travel and Entertainment budget things. She said we're budgeted for a pint but spending like we bought the whole pub, ya know! She was sayin the expenses are from amma amma your business credit card, ya know!"

"You've put me in an awkward position, Barney," Riich explained. "I'll tell you, but [*Riich leaned over and spoke in his 'just-between-us-girls voice'*] you can't tell anyone or you might get fired."

"What? Lord merciful clover fields! If I lose me job I won't have any money to keep up with me restaurant restoration hobby, ya know! I'm re-creatin a fish and chips pub in me backyard. Me lips are locked as if in the Bank Of Scotland vault."

"OK. I can't go into details, but about a month ago, Rolly Burnrock called me into his office. He hired me directly and we're close friends. He gave me a very confidential high level assignment and told me if I mentioned it to anyone he would fire me and the person I told. He said to put all the expenses related to the project on my company credit card, and that if anyone questioned the expenses to have them call him directly. I can give you his extension if you would like it, Barney."

"What? Amma amma amma amma amma."

"Look at the time. I've got to run to an important meeting. I'll be outside the bank most of the day on the special project. Thankkssssss."

March 2002 marked one year that Riich and Debbie had been seeing each other on a regular basis. Debbie had grown fond of Riich and enjoyed his company. Although not a materialistic person, she enjoyed the top-drawer lifestyle he showed her. She felt comfortable with Riich. He was attentive in bed, if somewhat mechanical. At times, he seemed distracted. They had started to enjoy love-making about six months earlier. Debbie's heart still belonged to Dan. She wondered if Riich could sense that she was not giving all of herself to their love-making, and maybe that was why he sometimes seemed like he was somewhere else. In the scheme of things that was secondary. Debbie believed Riich would provide financial security and a nice environment for her children.

Riich was very pleased with the progress on his special project. Debbie gave him what he needed to please Rolly and move his career forward: a woman and children. He even felt some love for her and was touched by her warmth and openness. If he wasn't so committed to his swinging lifestyle, Debbie might be the type of woman he would want.

The couple was married in April 2002. They had a private, low-key ceremony at Riich's house, with immediate family only. Riich invited Rolly, but he had a conflict that day.

By June, Riich was beginning to wonder why he had not been promoted to Senior Executive Deputy President. He had done what Rolly told him to do. To channel his frustrations, he devoted more and more of his time to High School Outreach.

Debbie began to get concerned about Riich after a series of curious events. She noticed that Riich's secretary pronounced his name as "Reach-ard," just like Gordon Mahlow at L'Fruitage had done. When she asked Riich about it, he said "Steffie has a speech impediment causing 'itch' to come out like 'eech.'" After getting to know Steffie over the phone, Debbie asked her about it one day. "Oh, I'm glad you noticed, Mrs. Shunk. That's the way Riich likes it pronounced. At first I pronounced it as Rich, but he had to correct me so much that he made up a sign with two i's and put it on my phone so I would remember to pronounce it as 'reach.' Please be sure to tell Riichard what a great job I'm doing saying his name the way he told me to."

Before they were married, Riich was attentive to Debbie, coming directly home from work most nights, sometimes bringing flowers or a bottle of wine. Things started to change in June. Riich told Debbie he had been put in charge of several "very important special projects" by the Chairman that would require him to lead a lot of "important meetings" and since this would be on top of everyone's existing responsibilities, he would be putting in a lot of late nights for the next several months.

The frequency of their love-making decreased when Riich started the 'special projects.' They typically had 3-4 sessions a week, but now Debbie was lucky to have 1 session. Riich would go straight to bed when he got home from work around 11:00 each night. Debbie would ask if he was hungry and Riich would explain that "I ordered food brought in for everyone because that keeps them motivated and you would not believe what a free meal means to lower level employees. A lot of employees volunteered to be on the projects because they want to work under me and get the food I order." Debbie occasionally snuggled with Riich. She thought it was curious that he did not get aroused, since, prior to the special project, he was quite virile. *Maybe he's under a lot of pressure from the projects*, she thought.

Debbie also was concerned by Riich's displays of dishonesty:

Like the time Riich took Debbie to a bar in West Chester before dinner. After Riich had three drinks, Debbie noticed that he kept turning around to look at the bartender. On about the sixth turnaround, the bartender was walking into the back carrying an empty bottle of scotch. Riich grabbed Debbie's arm and said, "Lets go we're going to be late" and pulled her out of the bar. "But Richard, we didn't pay," Debbie said. "I'm teaching that bartender a lesson in customer service." Riich answered. "If she wanted us to pay, she would have come over to collect. I'm teaching her a valuable lesson in leadership, Debra."

Or the time Riich took her to the King of Prussia Mall to shop at the big Mallstravaganza. Every store in the mall was offering merchandise at 30% off or more. A sale this big attracted a huge crowd. The Platinum, Double Platinum, Gold and Titanium Garages were all full. After almost 4 minutes of searching for a parking space, Riich got a huge smile on his face, said, "Guess what Daddy has?" pulled out a handicapped card, hung it on the rear-view mirror, and pulled into a handicapped space in front of Bloomingdales. "Are you injured, Richard?" Debbie said after seeing the card. "Of course not, Debra. I work out every day and am in exceptional shape. I was walking to my car last week after an important meeting and some handicapped person had left their window down with the card hooked to the rearview mirror, so I took it. I taught them a very important lesson about responsibility. These cards are valuable and they should be more careful about keeping them safe so they don't fall into the wrong hands. Besides, I've always believed that Senior Executives should have the best parking spots. Its not fair for handicapped people to get the best spots."

Riich was most proud of the lessons he taught store clerks. He liked to buy things on sale from boutiques or small stand-alone stores, then return the item after the sale was over. He would claim he lost his receipt and demand a full refund. He enjoyed browbeating young store clerks, believing he was helping toughen them up so they could deal with rude customers. He would whine and nag until the clerk gave a full price refund and agreed to give him a discount on regular-priced merchandise to make up for the inconvenience the store had caused an important Senior Executive like him.

I'm an Educator, Riich thought. *The work I do educating people on the realities of life is amazing. Think of how many clerks, bartenders and handicapped people are going to be better prepared to deal with liars and cheats because of the lessons I have taught.*

Critical mass occurred the day Debbie heard a faint buzzing sound inside the house, but could not figure out what it was. After a search, she discovered the buzzing was coming from a phone hidden in the back of Riich's walk-in closet. A pile of clothes was on the floor. Knowing how finicky Riich was about his clothes, Debbie guessed that he had used a pile of shirts and sweaters to hide the phone. The phone was pink and in the shape of a heart. There was a red flashing light on the phone. The phone buzzed again shortly after Debbie found it.

"Hiiii. How's our bitch Riich?" two voices called out in unison.

"What? Who is this?" Debbie asked.

"Well… who is this, the maid?" a man's voice said while a woman giggled.

"This is Mrs. Shunk, Richard's wife."

Debbie heard what sounded like a scream, followed by "OH MY GOODNESS!!! Riichard is married! Wait. I know. He's playing a joke on us. We're his friends Douglas and Breeta. We're calling to see if we're still on for tonight. Actually, you sound pretty hot. You can come with us if you like."

"How do you know my husband?" Debbie yelled.

"Hey… dial it back a notch, girl friend," Douglas said soothingly.

"Listen, you low-life pervert! Answer my question!" Debbie yelled again.

"Whoa… this ain't Crossfire, bitch." Douglas said and hung up.

Debbie felt flushed and sat on the floor. *Is this some type of sick joke? Are some of Richard's old college friends playing a game?*

Debbie pressed the red flashing button to hear the messages:

1. "Hiiii. Devonda here. Where are you, Pole Man? Call me back so we can interconnect. You got my numbers, stud."
2. "Hello Riich." [there was that 'reach' pronunciation again] "Amanda from Swingers' Palace. Bob and Terri really enjoyed

the hook-up with you and Nikkie the other night. They're coming again Thursday night and want to know if you can come too. The room you like with the smoked glass walls is available if you want it."

3. "Hi Riichard, it's James. I had a lovely evening last night. You were so gentle and the wacky dust was the best you've ever got. Can't wait to see you again soon. Bye."

4. "Listen up bitch! It's Douglas and Breeta. We're in the chamber and getting the toys ready for you. We got new chokers and straps. Call us back soon or you're gonna get some extra punishment when we get you here."

5. "Yo, it's Candyman. Your package is in. Bring $4,000 cash."

6. "Hey Riich, it's Nikkie. Bring me another friend over. James was a cutie. I think I broke him in good. I need more snow so get off your ass and make something happen. Oh…. Bring me the new Brittney CD too."

Hands shaking, Debbie called Riich at work. It was 4:50 in the afternoon.

"Good afternoon, First Galaxy, Riichard's office," Steffie said.

"Steffie, its Debbie Shunk. Please let me talk to Richard."

"Oh. He's…. Yes… he's in an important meeting," Steffie said.

"That's what you told me when I called earlier today. What time is the meeting over?"

"Oh well he's in a lot of different important meetings every day."

"This is very important. Please call him out of the meeting so I can speak with him."

"Well actually Mrs. Shunk, Riichard said this important meeting is out of the bank. He left here about 2:30 and said he would be in important meetings outside the bank until later this evening. He didn't leave a number where he could be reached."

"Why didn't you tell me that the first time?" Debbie said and hung up.

Debbie tried Riich on his cell phone, but it went right into voice mail. She felt like she had been kicked in the stomach. *I miss Dan so much. I can't believe this is happening.*

Debbie looked at her watch and realized she had been sitting in the closet for almost an hour. She went to the bathroom and splashed water on her face to clear her head. *What the hell should I do? Maybe there's an explanation for this or someone is playing a cruel joke. Should I talk to Richard about it? No... I've got to try to find out what's going on before I say anything. Maybe I'll try to follow him and see what's up. In the meantime, I'll keep eyes and ears wide open and play the role of "the good wife" to keep Richard, or whatever his name is, feeling like everything is ok at home.*

As the string of "important meetings out of the bank" continued, Debbie attempted to follow Riich. One day she saw him pick up a boy outside a local high school around 2:00 in the afternoon. They drove to a fancy neighborhood and pulled into a large garage at a very upscale house. The garage door closed as soon as Riich's car pulled in. The only sign of life Debbie saw was when a girl, who looked to be about 14, skipped down the driveway to check the mailbox. Once the girl got back inside, Debbie saw the shades get lowered in an upstairs room. Debbie parked near the house for another two hours and realized she had to get home to her kids. She decided to hire a private investigator to follow Riich and search his financial records, as she thought some professional expertise was needed. Within a month, the investigator reported back with evidence of daily liaisons with high school kids, trips to swingers clubs, hookups at motels with prostitutes and pickups from drug dealers. The private investigator suggested that Debbie visit a doctor to check for sexually transmitted diseases.

Regarding finances, Debbie was relieved to know that most of Richard's money was in joint accounts. She began moving the money into new accounts in her name only, and, in her best "good wife" voice offered to take care of all the bills and money things "since you're so busy at work and you get home so late from your important meetings that you shouldn't have to deal with that stuff."

Once Debbie had accumulated her evidence and moved most of Riich's money, she planned to go to a divorce lawyer. Thankfully and mercifully, her blood test came back clean, so at least she wouldn't be paying the ultimate price for her time with Riich. Riich's arrest made a conventional divorce unnecessary and actually put her in a better position to get the rest of his assets. *First on the list to go is that ugly Maplethorpe thing.*

By the time of Riich's arrest, Debbie had built up about $2 million in her own accounts. She couldn't believe that First Galaxy paid so much money to someone who did nothing. Who was minding the store at that place?

The experience with Riich hardened Debbie. Until she was rid of Riich, Debbie viewed herself as a cross between Kathleen Turner in

Body Heat and Sharon Stone in Basic Instinct, and was determined to pay back his emotional abuse by a factor of 10.

Debbie prepared to put the final pieces of her plan into action.

Chapter 21 – Act Now Think Later

"Hey JoAnna. What is this message from Sammy Shifster?" Tom Hughman called out to his secretary.

"He said he was calling to update you on a few things," JoAnna said.

Right, Tom thought. *The last time Sammy extended a professional courtesy to someone, dinosaurs were walking the earth.* Tom decided to talk with Ted Reilly before returning Sammy's call.

"Hey Reed. I've got a message to call Sammy Shifster. Anything I should know about? Oh…. OK, I understand. Thanks Ted."

"Go ahead and place the call JoAnna. Let me know when he's been on the line for about five minutes," Tom asked.

"Tom, Mr. Shifster is on your line. It's been five minutes, as you requested," JoAnna said.

"Sammy! What a pleasant surprise. What can I do for you?"

"OK Tom. Great. We need to crank up the marketing efforts and push harder to add more new group relationships to our production base. What do you think we should do first? I think we should do both. What do you think. My guys are ready to work 24/7, kick in the after-burners, hit the nitrous button, go for the gold… er platinum. The opportunities in front of us are a slam-dunk and we need to hold serve before SuiteBanque goes deep on us. We've got to act like its late in the 4th quarter with the bases loaded. Lately it seems like the checkered flag is waving and we're still at mid-field. You agree that we should super-size the marketing plans and turbo-charge the selling efforts?"

"What does Ted think about this?" Tom asked.

"On board. 100% committed. Locked and loaded. Ready for the starting gun to fire. Let's go with a 75% ramp-up in marketing. Take the hand-cuffs off, raise the bar, run with the ball," Sammy said.

"You have a point, Sammy. We need the resources to get things done. Everything was running well when Barney O'Farkle was in Production. It looks like we put a wrench in the spokes, put on the brakes, let air out of the tires, took a wrong turn, threw a brick at the buzzer, struck out, fumbled the ball, didn't put enough coal in the fire, by taking Barney away from a job he clearly had mastered. Let me talk with Ted, but I think to do your plan the right way we need Barney at the helm to steer the ship, quarterback the team, take the bull by the horns, tighten our laces, pull ourselves up by the bootstraps. I'll have Barney give you a shout right off and start scheduling some meetins."

"Tom, before you rush off half-assed, I want to talk with my guys to size up the opportunities. Let me explore a Plan B. I understand Barney is in a mission-critical position and can't be moved. Let's put this on the back burner and get our ducks in a row. You're a good guy Tom, but sometimes you move too fast. And lighten up on the metaphors. I'll get back to you," Sammy said and hung up.

Tom had just hung up the phone when Breeze Penner burst into his office. Breeze was sweating and the color had drained from his face.

"Hey Tom, got a minute?" Breeze said while wiping his face with a handful of napkins. Unknown to Breeze, his face was dotted with napkin pieces.

"You OK, LQ? What's up?"

"I just got out of Rolly's office. He made me wait in his conference room for almost two hours, then came in, slammed the door, and started screaming about his Faberge egg. Said he found it smashed to pieces on the floor of his office. He said if he didn't have a replacement within forty-eight hours, I would be fired, my house and car repossessed and he'd have my brain cut out if I had one."

"How did you respond, Breeze?" Tom asked.

"Didn't have a chance to respond, Tom. Soon as he was done screaming, he left the room. I can contact some of the New York auction houses to see what's available. Given the cost, you and Ted are going to have to sign off."

"Have you lost your mind, Breeze?" Tom cut in. "Do you know what those things cost? They're around $10 million EACH! The one in his office was a gift to the company from our founding owner's collection. It was valued at $500,000 back then. Have Security run the video tapes from Rolly's office and find out what happened. Then file an insurance claim. This company has far better use for $10 million than buying another egg."

"I agree, Tom. Let me know what Rolly says when you talk with him." Breeze said.

"No need, since you'll be there, by yourself, to update the Chairman. Let me know what he says." Tom said to end the conversation.

Less than one hour later, Tom's phone rang with the *priority tone* signaling it was The Chairman.

"Tom Hughm"

"WHEN WAS THE BOARD MEETING?" Rolly screamed into the phone.

"Which Board Meeting are you referring to?" Tom asked, wondering what the hell Rolly was talking about.

"THE ONE WHERE YOU WERE ELECTED CHAIRMAN! I AM THE CHAIRMAN OF THIS COMPANY AND WHEN I TELL YOU TO DO SOMETHING, YOU DO IT! ARE WE CLEAR? YOU HAVE NO AUTHORITY TO BLOCK THE PURCHASE OF THE EGG!"

"Rolly, I'm not aware of what Breeze said to you. Breeze was very upset and asked for my advice, which was to begin the insurance claim process."

"WE DON'T HAVE TIME FOR THAT SHIT! I WANT A REPLACEMENT EGG IN 48...47 HOURS!"

"We'll be in a more favorable position with the insurance company if we put through a vandalism claim before purchasing a new egg. I suggested that Breeze pull the security tapes for your office to see what happened." Tom said.

"I WILL NOT INSULT THE MEMORY OF OUR FOUNDING OWNER BY TURNING THIS INTO A BUREAUCRATIC CRAWL MISSION! SKIP THE INSURANCE BULL SHIT AND GET ME MY EGG. NOW IT'S 46½ HOURS! SINCE YOU STUCK YOUR NOSE IN THIS, I'M MAKING YOU RESPONSIBLE FOR GETTING THE EGG."

"I told you how I would handle it; through the insurance process. I'll proceed with that approach. As the second-ranking officer in this company, I am obligated to give you my best counsel, which is to invest the insurance proceeds in the business and forego another egg." Tom said and moved the receiver away from his ear.

To Tom's relief, the only sound he heard was the slamming of the phone, followed by a distant sound of breaking glass. Tom made a quick voice note to his secretary: "JoAnna, please make a trip to Pierre Wonders and buy a Faberge Egg-like piece. Don't spend more than $25. Thanks."

Chapter 22 – Circle Of Ideas

Grip Grayson was a Man Of Ideas. He had so much intellectual power that he felt compelled to share his brilliance with others. Grip's favorite forum for launching his ideas was at his daily staff meetings, where he had a captive audience.

Grip's staff meetings started at rolling 3-hour intervals: 7:00AM on Monday, 10:00 Tuesday, 1:00 Wednesday, 4:00 Thursday, and 7:00PM Friday. Monday and Friday meetings were 60 minutes; other days they were 30 minutes, unless Grip extended the time for an idea that could not wait 26½ hours until the next meeting. Starting early on Monday and ending late on Friday meant Grip provided a weekly *Circle of Ideas* to his staff.

Monday and Friday meetings were with Grip's direct reports only. Tuesday through Thursday, the entire Certificates & Degrees staff was invited. Grip was an inclusive executive and wanted as many employees as possible to hear his ideas.

"Shit, its 10:00 already," Yale Sayle said to his cube neighbor, Wendy Kreckly.

"Great. It's Tuesday, so we have to go to Dimy's meeting," Wendy said.

Grip's favorite line was "do it my way." He said it so much that the C&D staff called him Dimy.

"OK group let's get started we only have 30 minutes and there's a lot to do," Grip said in his rapid-fire montone. "Today I have morale building ideas. Recognition is a good way to build morale. We need something to complement First Galaxy's structured recognition programs, many of which were my ideas. Good ideas don't happen according to a schedule so why should recognition follow a schedule?

"My idea is an "*Employee of the Moment*" award, to recognize the great things employees do throughout the day. For example, last week my secretary was running a long copy job for me, so while the copy machine was running, she hustled to the café and got me some coffee. Or what about you, Sally? The other day I saw you using an extra long straw to drink your soda. By using a long straw, you could suck on your drink and keep both hands busy on your keyboard. And let's not skip Amy Wileskiew. Realizing her last name is difficult to spell, Amy told her colleagues to send her inter-office mail addressed to Amy "W" to save them from having to look up her name. Can you imagine how much time that will save across the company? Finally, the man of the moment, Vito O'Madso. Vito was here late one day last week, around 8:30PM if my memory is correct. He used the speakerphone to say 'good-night' to his kids, so he could pound the keyboard *and* fulfill his parental responsibilities at the same time. What a great example of balancing work and family, Vito! Sally, Amy, and Vito have earned the *Employee of the Moment* award."

Grip handed Sally, Amy, and Vito a blank award sheet, then filled in their names and his signature.

<u>Employee Of The Moment</u>

Awarded to _____

To recognize that little ideas add up to a LOT!

Presented on _____ **by Grip Grayson**

Expires 1-month from the day listed.

"Hold them up so the whole group can see," Grip beamed. "What do you guys think of my idea?"

"It seems like a good concept, Grip, but I wonder if it would make it even better if the person's name and the date were typed on the award," Judy Culson said.

"I thought of that and think it's more personal this way," Grip said. Let's do it my way and see how it goes. Any other thoughts?"

"Why does it expire? It's like you did the good idea and then it's like taken away," Bretna Spreegs asked.

"I thought of that and want to keep everyone motivated to earn more awards. Let's do it my way and see how it goes. OK, 30 minutes are up. Back to work."

Chapter 23 – Confident And Competent

Gina Stream was excited. So excited that she wore a charcoal gray suit to work instead of her trademark midnight black. It was her first day in the office since her promotion, vacation to the Outer Banks, holiday in Europe, and Management Summit in Hawaii. She made a mental note to make sure her new business cards were ready.

Gina was in at her usual time, 7:00AM, and noted that none of the Banker Market staff were in yet. *You'd think they were ahead of Plan,* she sniffed. Gina's thoughts were interrupted by the phone.

"Gina Stream."

"Good morning, Gina. This is June, in Ted Reilly's office. Ted would like to meet with you at 7:45. Are you available?"

"I'll be there," Gina said and hung up.

So much for getting a jump-start on the week. Maybe he wants to give me an atta-girl on my first official day as a Senior Executive. I wonder if Rolly Burnrock will be there. Maybe they have an Induction Ceremony. I hope Trina will be there. But not her loser husband. What a load he is! Did she marry him because she lost a bet or something? It would be real cool if they give me one of those gold-lined leather portfolios with a page detailing my new salary and bonus. Oh, that's silly; the portfolio will be platinum-lined, not gold. I bet they have a checklist so I can pick out the company car and the options I want. I hope I can get heated seats. I wonder how many stock options I'll get. Someone from Interior Management will probably be there so I can pick out furniture and art work for my new office. I wonder if my office will have a private bathroom. Well… time to go. Need to remember to act surprised.

"Good morning, Gina. Come on in my conference room," Ted said, greeting Gina with a handshake.

"Good morning, Ted. How was your weekend?" Gina said. *How much small talk are we going to do? I'm too busy to bull-shit all day. Wait a minute! Where is everyone? What about my Induction Ceremony? Where's the guy with the information about my car with the heated seats?*

"It was great. Thanks for asking. So today is your first day back in the office after your vacations and the Management Summit. A lot has happened during the time you were away. You've been at First Galaxy a little over two years, so you know how fast we move. Sometimes we move so fast we need to make adjustments along the way.

"Rolly, Tom and I have a lot of responsibilities, and the most important is to ensure our employees are treated in accordance with our core values. Recent events at the company have lead Rolly, Tom and I to do some self-reflection on how well we've been doing with this responsibility, and there are some key areas where we can do better.

"So how does this involve you? Gina, we believe you can be a future leader at this company. Tom is very pleased with the support you've provided the past two years. We believe the best course for your development is to continue as Tom's Budget Analyst. Your technical skills are solid. We'd like you to focus on developing your leadership and people skills. You've done very well as an Analyst, Gina, and you need to gain an appreciation for the efforts of others. Apparently your introduction to the Banker Market did not go well. Use it as a learning experience and a baseline for improving your interpersonal skills.

"We're going to put your promotion on hold. Nothing was announced throughout the company, so to my knowledge, no one knows about it. Tom is going to discuss a leadership development program for you. Why don't you return to your office to let this sink in, and then give Tom a call when you're ready. Thanks, Gina."

Ted shook Gina's hand and returned to his office. *That wasn't so bad. Better a little awkwardness now than a big blow-up down the road,* Ted thought.

"June. Please call Mort Grack and ask him to meet with me in thirty minutes. Go ahead and start placing the other phone calls we discussed earlier." Ted said.

A few minutes later, June said, "Ted, John Billoughs is on your line."

"Good morning, John. How was your weekend?"

"Good morning, Ted. It was fine, thanks. What can I do for you?" John Billoughs was the Chief Financial Officer at Shifster Production Services. His job was to watch Sammy's money as if each dollar was an endangered species.

"I took a look at the invoices SPS sent us over the past year and I know I'm not a numbers guy, but I'm having a hard time matching up the production volumes you're billing us for with the volumes I have on my own reports. I'd like you to re-run the invoices to see if you come up with the same numbers."

"This is the way we've been doing it for a long time, Ted. If I've got to re-run the invoices, I'm going to need to have people work overtime and even then it's going to take at least a week," John replied.

"One week is fine. I'll look for them next Monday. Send them down via FedEx Platinum-Time Delivery Service. Thanks for your help, John," Ted said and hung up.

"June, go ahead and place the next call," Ted said.

"Blue Morock is on your line, Ted."

"Big Blue! Big Blue! How are you?" Ted said to the Director Of Universal Relationship Development at SPS. Blue had recently been promoted from Director of Global Relationship Development. He felt confined by the word "Global" and thought "Universal" more appropriately reflected the scope of his talents.

"On top of the universe, Ted! I'm pumped this morning. Set a new bench-press record today, 275 lbs, then ran 4 miles, all before breakfast."

"Very impressive, Blue. I know its getting late in the year, but I want you to tweak some of your production goals. Let's do four fewer Certificates & Degrees production set-ups and do... let's see... let's do three more Retail set-ups and two more Mega Conglomerates. As pumped as you sound, I'll bet you can do it before the day is over!"

"Hey, you know our slogan: Confident And Competent. Are you sure about those changes, Ted? The lead time on Retail and Mega set-ups is 8-9 months. There's not enough time left in the year to hit those goals."

"I don't want to micro-manage your efforts, Blue. You're Mr. Universe, aren't you? I'm meeting with Rolly later today and will let him know you agreed to the goal changes. Thanks, Blue."

"I'm off, June. Do we have time for one more?" Ted asked.

"I think so, Ted. Mort Grack will be here in ten minutes. I'll get Matla Ripcut for you."

"Good morning Matla. This is Ted Reilly at First Galaxy. It's a pleasure to meet you over the phone," Ted said to the manager of contract processing at SPS.

"Yes, Mr. Reilly. What is it I can be of service to you today?"

"I was wondering if you could do a favor for me, Matla."

"Yes, Mr. Reilly. I would be of happiness for helping to you."

"I'd like to see a comparison of the contract production reports month-over-month going back for three years," Ted said.

"You mean it is what you would like would be to see how over each month for last three year how contracts moved through process?" Matla asked.

"Yes, that's it exactly. Thanks, Matla."

"Can be done with a lot of much time. Will need to do overtime hours to be paid for staff to do work. When need to have the reports?"

"No rush. Next week would be fine, perhaps by Tuesday."

"Will do our best for meeting your request. If not able will let you be informed by ending of this week." Matla replied.

"Thanks, Matla. Good bye." Ted said and hung up.

"Hey June. I have a weather update for you. Hurricane Sammy is going to blow in some time later today. Wait until he's died down to a Tropical Storm, which should be about four calls, before you get me." Ted said.

"You're on a roll today, Ted," June replied. "Mort Grack is here. I'll ask him to go into your conference room."

"I'll meet with him in my office. Send him in. Thanks."

"Good to see you Mort. Have a seat," Ted said.

"Hello, Ted," Mort replied.

"Rolly, Tom and I want you to know we appreciate the leadership you've demonstrated during your time in the Banker Market. It's clear you have a good team and you're the guy to get Bankers back on track. Effective today, you are the new Director of the Banker Market and are promoted to Executive Deputy President. It's my pleasure to be the first to congratulate you.

"Last year, Bankers was the #2 account generator for the company. Your mission is to get back to that level and do it in a way that supports and develops your employees. Bankers will continue to report to David Gando. David will announce your new role to the group once you're back upstairs. OK. I don't want to hold you up any longer. Go get 'em!" Ted said to end the meeting.

"Thank you, Ted. I appreciate your confidence. We have a great team in Bankers and we're going to show you what we can do." Mort said, then left the office.

Chapter 24 – Debbie Doin' The Right Thing

"Rolly, Debbie Shunk has called three times. I told her you would not be available for most of the day, but she sounds very upset." Helen said to Rolly as he entered his office.

"I wonder what she wants. I'll talk to her now if she's there." Rolly said.

"I think she just wants a shoulder to cry on. I'll get her on the line for you."

"Hello Debbie. We are all shocked and saddened by the recent events. How are you holding up?" Rolly said to open the call.

"Oh, Mr. Burnrock, it's just terrible," Debbie said, sobbing loudly. "I…. I don't know what I'm going to do. Richard provided all the financial support and managed all the money. I don't even know if we have any money." Debbie cried.

"I understand. I'm very sorry for the pain you're going through. I feel somewhat responsible. If we had given Richard more support, maybe he would not have strayed so much. I would like to personally fund college savings accounts for your children and pay off the balance on your mortgage. That will eliminate two major financial burdens you would be facing. Is there anything else I can do?" Rolly asked.

Shit! Debbie thought. *My plan worked too well. I was just hoping for an easy $50,000 or so, paid by First Galaxy. That's the least they could do for putting up with a corrupt piece of shit like Richard. I can't take this man's own money, especially not the sums he's talking about. What* *an irony... the last thing I want to do is become a lying sack of shit like Richard.*

"I'm touched beyond words by your very generous offer, Mr. Burnrock. I don't think I need any money. Everything has happened so suddenly, maybe we have more than I thought. I may have over-reacted because I'm upset by everything that's happened. I remember seeing some bank statements somewhere in Richard's files, so that would be a good place for me to look first. I guess I just wanted a shoulder to cry on. I'm sorry for bawling like an idiot. Your generous offer reminded me of how lucky I really am. I'm sure we're going to be fine." Debbie said.

"You're sure? I'll keep my offer on the table for a month. If you change your mind or your circumstances change, let me know and the money is yours. Bye." Rolly said and hung up.

That was close! Debbie thought. To think I almost took advantage of that man's generosity. That doesn't mean I'm not going to proceed with the last part of my plan to make sure Richard is down and stays down.

Debbie had put together copies of the photos and other evidence the Private Investigator gathered while following Richard. She put one set in a large envelope with an anonymous typed letter of explanation and sent it to the local newspaper, The Delaware Times. This would make a great complement to their coverage of Richard's crimes and would provide a nice introduction for Richard to the prison guards and his fellow inmates.

Maybe the courts didn't given him a life sentence, but once this information becomes public, he'll carry a reputation so bad that even he won't be able to slither away from it. He'll be as welcome in "normal *society" as someone with leprosy and raging herpes. Moving to Wilmington did expose us to more excitement; too much excitement. My $2 million will go a long way in Milford, which is where the kids and I are headed just as soon as I unload this disgusting house, the perverted art work and the gaudy furnishings. I'll look on* <u>www.rich_perverts_with_bad_taste.com</u> *to find a buyer for this trash.*

Chapter 25 – The Sky Clears

"Ted, your weather forecast was correct. Mr. Shifster called nine times so far today. The last time he called, he seemed to be losing a little steam. He said he would call back at 5:15, about ten minutes from now. If he sounds calm, I'll put him through." June said to Ted Reilly.

"Thanks, June. I'll be ready. I hope you didn't get blasted too badly today."

"Wait… here he is now. I'll put him through."

"Sammy. How's it going?" Ted said.

"What the hell is going on down there, Ted? [Loud crinkling noises from a chip bag]. Has the place turned into an insane asylum? The other day, Tom Hughman calls and goes on for fifteen minutes with a bunch of idiotic sports metaphors, and now you're turning my company upside down with a bunch of pain-in-the-ass requests! This is my company and I set the priorities. If you want to change the goals or get some reports, you go through me." [More chip bag noises, followed by the sound of a handful of chips being shoved into Sammy's mouth].

"Let me make sure I understand. What exactly has you upset?" Ted asked.

"That you're [cough, cough, cough]… hold on I need some water…. going directly to my staff and wasting their time and my money with a bunch of changes and crap when you should be talking to me!" [more bag rattling].

"So, your view is that all changes or requests should be directed to whom?"

"All of it goes through me. No one else. Clear as glass."

"OK, I think I'm starting to understand. Maybe we should start the new system right now. I have a request to make to you." Ted said.

"That's the spirit. Shoot."

"Stop calling me, Tom and my Market Directors ten times a day! If I give you an answer you don't like, have the balls to tell me. Don't call Tom or a Market Director and try to blow it by them. Back off, Sammy!"

"Take it easy, Ted. Let's give your way a try and see how it goes." Sammy said, then hung up as the receiver slipped out of his hand from all the grease and nacho coating.

Chapter 26 – Team Work

Grip Grayson knew that a well-rounded Executive had to be on top of current events and trends. He subscribed to magazines and journals that cut a wide swath: *The Economist, Forbes, Jet, DownBeat, Federal Reserve Bank Beige Book, Entrepreneur, Human Resources Executive, Institutional Investor, Spin, Ebony,* and more. The magazines were kept on the table outside his office for all to see.

Grip believed he had a responsibility to share his ideas with all areas of First Galaxy, not just the C&D Market. To communicate his ideas with his fellow Senior Executives, he created the *Grip-A-Gram*; a one-page note with the latest brilliant thinking from Grip Grayson. He sent out about 2-3 per week. Most of the recipients called them GAGs.

On this particular Friday afternoon in mid-October, Grip's focus was on morale. He was so pumped by his *Employee of the Moment* program that he wanted to get more ideas into circulation. He sent a *Grip-A-Gram* to the Director of Morale Enhancement with a brain dump of his latest thinking:

Grip-A-Gram   *from the desk of <u>Grip Grayson</u>*

Barney:

Congratulations on your new position in Morale Enhancement. I spend a lot of time on morale. I've jotted down some ideas for your consideration. They're slam-dunks:

- Free coffee for employees on their birthday (limited to 1 12oz cup)
- Let strong performers use their manager's office for a day, to make them feel important
- Offer reduced parking rates in the garage for employees who arrive before 7:00AM and leave after 7:00PM
- Program the soda vending machines to give random free cans of soda, say 1 in every 500 cans.
- A new savings plan: Give a $25 Savings Bond in exchange for giving up a vacation day
- For Top Performers: When they move to a different department, retire their phone extension similar to what is done for professional athletes' uniform number.

I'd be happy to discuss these with you. If we do it my way, these ideas will be a big success. I'll wait a few days for your reaction and then forward this to Ted and Tom.

Grip

After reading the Federal Reserve Beige Book, he fired off a *Grip-A-Gram* to Wallace Malvagio, Chief Financial Officer:

Grip-A-Gram   *from the desk of <u>Grip Grayson</u>*

Wallace:

- The latest Fed Beige Book shows production of durable goods is growing faster than expected in the mid-west.
- Have you adjusted the 2005 Plan for this?
- I think we should increase credit lines for people living in the mid-west so they can purchase more appliances. What do you think?

I'd be happy to discuss this with you. If we do it my way, these ideas will be a big success. I'll wait a few days for your reaction and then forward this to Ted and Tom.

Grip

Friday at 7:00PM. Time for our week-ending Staff Meeting. Today is a good day to discuss my productivity improvement ideas, Grip thought.

"Hey Katie, Dimy just called. It's time for his Staff Meeting." Reeve McMack said to his next-door cube mate, Katie Aighton. "Let's get May and get started. If we're lucky, we'll be home by 8:30." Katie, Reeve, and May Beely were Grip's three direct reports.

"OK guys let's get started." Grip said once the group had gathered. "How did we do this week?"

"We're having challenges with some partners to get access to their full marketing list," Katie said. "More and more companies are telling us that people are complaining about getting so many credit card offers, and they're starting to resist sharing their lists. My contact at Shifster Production Services keeps hammering me to do more mailings, but I think we might be getting diminishing returns."

"What do you suggest we do?" Grip asked.

"I've been talking about it with my team and we've come up with a few ideas." Katie said, then proceeded to summarize the ideas.

"Excellent ideas, Katie. Have any of the other Markets faced this challenge? Do we know how they addressed it? If Shifster is pestering the other Markets as well, we may need to let Ted Reilly know. Grip asked.

"Let me look into that, Grip. That would be good information to know before we make a decision. Thanks." Katie said.

"How are we doing on our new programs? I'm particularly interested in CAM, the Center for Auto Mechanics. That's the largest new C&D group this year." Grip said.

"So far so good," Reeve replied. "The Lug Nut mailing is off to a fast start. Response rate so far is 1.2% on a volume of 300,000 pieces. We have one more mailing scheduled in the 4th quarter and are finalizing the 2005 marketing plans as we speak."

"This seems like a great program for magazine ads in auto-related magazines. Seems like we should be advertising heavily. I can go get my copy of Car & Driver if you like." Grip said.

"We've discussed the possibility of magazine ads with CAM. They're concerned about diluting the value of a CAM degree if we do general advertising. They only want CAM students and graduates carrying the CAM card in their wallets. Seems like a reasonable point." Reeve responded, bracing for a *do it my way* comment.

"If we do it my way, we can put on a lot more accounts and that means more money for CAM. Can we do it my way and see how it works?" Grip said.

"That's a great idea, Grip and it might be even more powerful if we keep it in reserve for when the program is more mature. Since the list is fresh and response rates are strong, I'd prefer to focus on the group's list for now and consider complementing the list with magazine ads down the road. Perhaps by that time, the group will be more open to the idea." Reeve said.

"I thought of that. That's a good idea. Let's do it that way for now. Good work, Reeve. You thought it through well and it sounds like you're building a good relationship with the group. Thanks." Grip said. "I had some productivity improvement ideas to share, but why don't we table them until Monday. You guys and your teams had a great week. Go ahead and enjoy your weekends." Grip said.

"Is Dimy sniffing glue?" May asked Reeve and Katie on the way out.

"Don't knock it," Katie replied. "I heard that word came down from on high that the senior execs need to focus more on leadership stuff and treating employees the right way. Maybe he's making an effort. He actually had some good input and he listened to our ideas. I'll take that any day."

"You're right, Katie. Hopefully this is a new trend. It'll make things a lot more enjoyable around here if it is." May said.

Chapter 27 – Movin' On Up

Grace Grack enjoyed her position as Senior Property Manager for Balsa Property Management, but was tired of explaining to new clients that the company was named after Barry Balsa and the name had nothing to do with the type of wood used to build their properties.

"Good morning, this is Grace Grack." Grace said when her phone rang.

"YO! Yeah, I were just promoted at where I work and I want to upgrade my single-wide trailer to double-wide. You able arrangement that?" the caller asked.

"Sir, Balsa Property Management just achieved Platinum Level ranking from Premier Real Estate Magazine. Our line of properties *starts* at triple-wide. If you is interest in one a them we can arrangement that." Grace said.

"I got me enough dead presidents to do some kind a monthly payment round $175 dollar. You got triple-wide for that money I might take a look, longs it got that fake panelin inside the bedroom. You sound hot. You come out and show me the unit yourself and maybe I show you my unit at same time."

"That sounds great, sir. I hook up with strangers at our properties all the time to test the bedroom floors for creaks. It's just one of the extra services we provide here at Balsa. So what time you want to meet, Mr. Grack?"

"How did you know it was me, Babe?"

"Probably because we've been married for ten years and you suck at voice impressions. You made me nervous at first, because I actually

167

did meet someone for sex last week, and I thought they were calling back." Grace said.

"That's good, now I don't feel so guilty about banging that summer intern on the conference room table last night. Alright. I've got great news. I was just promoted to Executive Deputy President and Director of the Banker Market!"

"SWEET! I am so proud of you! It's about f-in time. You sure earned it. Let's go out and celebrate tonight. And let's celebrate at lunch. I'm going to book a room at the Hotel Pierre and have sex with the newest EDP at First Galaxy!"

"Damn, I'm so excited I don't think I'll need to take my usual triple-dose of Viagra. No more mac and cheese out of a can for us. From now on, we're buying the good stuff that comes in a box! You know, the biggest thrill for me is that I get to share this with you. I'm so lucky to have a wife as beautiful inside and out as you. You know, my heart still jumps each time I see you."

"And you're my king, Mort. I wouldn't want to change anything about you or our life, especially now that we're going to upgrade to boxed mac and cheese. I'll meet you in the hotel lobby at 12:30."

As Mort was walking back to his department, he was faced with an AWKWARD MOMENT: Gina Stream was coming down the hallway towards him.

Shit! How uncomfortable is this! Is it too late to 'remember' something I left at the other end of the hallway and run in the other direction? Mort thought to himself.

Gina was equally happy to see Mort walking towards her. *Pile of shit! The prick has probably been waiting there all morning to 'run into me.' What a classless moron loser. Maybe I'll go knee him in the balls. Oh, can't do that… it might hurt my career.*

"Hey, Gina. Sorry we're not going to have the chance to work together. Do you feel as awkward as I do? Walking on hot coals would be more comfortable than this. I'm sorry for what happened to you, but it's no reflection on you and I, since we never really were in the same group." Mort said.

"Thanks Mort. I appreciate that. I have to admit, when I first saw you walking towards me, I was not full of good cheer. But, what you said is right. Congratulations on your promotion. I'll see you later." Gina said and continued back to her office.

Now I know why Tom put that Dale Carnegie Program brochure on my desk last week. I guess he was trying to tell me something. I know a few people who went through the program and it really helped them. I'll look into it. Gina thought.

Chapter 28 – Get A *Grip-A-Gram*

A few days after he sent the *Grip-A-Gram* about economic growth in the mid-west to Wallace Malvagio, Grip received a reply via interoffice mail.

Mr. Grayson: The Office of Wallace Malvagio received a note from you regarding the 2005 Plan. Mr. Malvagio's secretary forwarded your note to the Planning Director, who forwarded it to the Planning Manager, who forwarded it to the Planning Analyst, who forwarded it to me, the Planning Input Specialist. The Planning and Control Division already reflects all relevant economic and market information in the Annual Plan. We deal with very large dollar amounts so a temporary change in production of washers and dryers is not something we consider to be relevant or material. The Plan, which has been approved by Mr. Malvagio, will remain as constructed.

I trust this puts your question to rest.

Fred Blake
Planning Input Specialist

Doesn't sound like they disagree. I'll pass my idea to Credit. Grip sent a *Grip-A-Gram* to Michael Koureouli, the Director of Credit, the area that established customer credit lines:

Grip-A-Gram from the desk of <u>Grip Grayson</u>

Michael:

- The latest Fed Beige Book shows production of durable goods is growing faster than expected in the mid-west.
- I think we should increase credit lines for people living in the mid-west since they are clearly purchasing more appliances.
- I ran my idea by Wally Malvagio and he's on board. What do you think?

I'd be happy to discuss this with you. If we do it my way, this will be a big success. I'll wait a few days for your reaction and then forward this to Ted and Tom.

Grip

It's almost 10:00. Just enough time to get another Grip-A-Gram out before my staff meeting.

Grip-A-Gram from the desk of <u>Grip Grayson</u>

Giovanni Pasterana – Director Of Building Management:
Percy Formmeiu – Director Of Personnel

This idea benefits both of your areas. We can improve productivity and reduce company expenses by implementing the following ideas:

1. Put all conference room lights on a timer that automatically turns lights off after 10 minutes/5 minutes/1 minute. After the final 1 minute, they cannot be turned back on for 1 hour. Ensures meetings will be more productive and lights will not be kept on needlessly.
2. Same concept, only for heating/cooling. Without light and air, meetings will be shorter and participants will stay focused. The policy needs to prohibite the use of flashlights and portable fans.

I'd be happy to discuss my ideas with you. If we do it my way, these ideas will significantly boost worker productivity. I'll wait a few days for your reaction and then forward this to Ted and Tom.

Grip

"OK let's get started." Grip said once the group had gathered. "We're going to use a new approach for these meetings starting today. Katie, Reeve, and May will rotate as the meeting leader for our Tuesday and Thursday meetings from now on. That means they will select the topics to be discussed. Katie, I know I'm catching you off guard, but why don't you run today's meeting?"

"Sure, Grip. Thanks. Let's do brief updates from each of our areas. I'll get things started with a marketing update." Katie said.

For the next 45 minutes, the group had an interactive discussion and identified several opportunities to work together more effectively.

"That was terrific." Grip said at the meeting conclusion. "Does anyone have ideas for other things we can do in these meetings?"

"Um, I have one thought to toss out." May said. "Would it be ok to start these meetings at the same time each day? The reason I ask is that a lot of us are in other meetings throughout the week and the different start times mean we aren't able to go to other meetings."

"You don't like my *Circle of Ideas?*" Grip said.

"Not at all." May replied. *And I do mean Not At All, you idiot.* "Since we're making some changes to these meetings, I just thought I'd toss it out for consideration."

"I had thought of that. Let me think about this, May." Grip said, leaning back in his chair and looking to the heavens as if deciding whether to order a nuclear strike on an enemy country. "If we do it my way, I think we'll get good results, but, maybe we do spend too much time in meetings around here. As you know, productivity is one of my passions and if you're telling me our productivity will be better if meetings start at the same time each day, then we should give it a try. I just sent some huge ideas for enhancing meeting productivity to Personnel and Building Management, so this is a good time to think about our own meetings.

"I have an idea: Let's start the meetings at the same time each day and reduce the number of meetings to one per week with the full department and two per week with my direct reports. If we do it my way, we'll improve information flow, boost productivity and save time. Great. Back to work." Grip said and the meeting was over.

Grip had a message to call Ted Reilly when he returned to his office.

"Hello Ted, this is Grip."

"SLIC Grip! How are you?" Ted said, referring to the SLIC Program, *Study... Learn... Identify... Contribute,* Grip developed in Quality & Accuracy. "The November Special Morning Management Meeting is in two weeks and we'd like you to present some of your latest ideas. We need more big thinkers around here and you might inspire us to kick-start the way we do things."

"Thank you, Ted. I'll put together a 10-minute overview." Grip said.

"How are the C&D results looking?"

"We're looking good, Ted. The team is really clicking and coming up with some great marketing ideas and group relationship strategies. I'm proud of my team. We have a good shot to exceed our plan this year."

"Good to hear. Keep it up. Thanks, Grip."

Chapter 29 – A New Day

Rolly was in a good mood for the November Special Morning Management Meeting. He was going to deliver a "GO" message to his executives: Shape up or Get Out!

Rolly had set an admission price for the November SMMM, proceeds to be used to set up a fund for the families victimized by Riichard Shunk. Rolly was going to match the proceeds himself. He estimated that at least $1 million would be raised.

The admission price was "optional," but each attendee was required to sign in and indicate the amount they paid for their ticket. Anyone who did not pay their admission would receive a follow-up phone call from Rolly.

Rolly opened the meeting at 7:30AM on the dot and had the doors to the House of Cards auditorium locked. "Good morning. This is the start of a new day at First Galaxy. I will announce several changes today. The first change was just implemented: Show up on time or get out! Ted will introduce our speakers, and I will make some remarks at the end of the meeting."

"Thank you, Rolly. Our first speaker is Breeze Penner."

"Thank you, Ted. Good morning. I've been working with Wallace Malvagio on some expense reduction opportunities. We call it the NoMo Program:

- Automobiles – No more company cars, no more company-paid gasoline, maintenance, repairs or body work. Estimated annual savings: $1.5 million.

- Food – No more breakfast, lunch and snacks paid by First Galaxy. Starting today, you'll pay for your food like everyone else. Estimated annual savings: $2.5 million.
- Travel – No more First class travel. No more car services. Hotel suites will no longer be allowed. Florist, grooming, massage and fitness costs will no longer be reimbursed. Estimated annual savings: $5 million.

"Wallace wants to bill everyone for past use of company cars and all the other things covered in the NoMo Program. Anyone with complaints about the program will get an invoice from Wallace. NoMo will save First Galaxy about $10 million per year."

"Thank you, Breeze. Next, Grip Grayson will present some ideas on challenges and opportunities facing our company. I encourage each of you to **F**ocus, **U**nderstand and **C**oncentrate on Grip's remarks."

As Grip walked to the podium, Ted passed him a slip of paper with *Find....Understand...Contribute* on it, and whispered, "Don't FUC this up, Grip."

Grip's face turned crimson, but he shook it off so he could give his presentation.

"Good morning. I'm going to present some of my ideas on a passion of mine: Employee Productivity. My productivity ideas can be summed up in three words: Time Is Money. Every minute of employee time we free up is an additional minute they can spend on behalf of First Galaxy. Every minute we free up is worth about $10,000 for First

Galaxy. I call these my *Fingers On Keyboard* ideas, since our goal is to get everyone into work and at their computers as quickly as possible:

- *Use slip-on shoes.* Slip-ons will get employees dressed and on the way to work faster each morning. Shoe laces take too long. Clip-on ties for men are also suggested.
- *Designate a "PC Starter"* in each department to get in 10 minutes early every day to power-up every computer, eliminating time people spend waiting for their computer to boot up.
- *"Drive-Time Conference Calls."* Have conference calls with your employees during their commute. Get all the "good mornings" and social niceties out of the way before arriving at work.
- *Auto-PC logoff after 30 seconds of inactivity.* If 30 seconds go by with no keyboard activity, computers will shut down. This will keep employees fingers on keyboards. I've prototyped some posters to support my idea: "Fingers On Keyboards: Stop Thinking And Start Working".
- Put up a *Keystroke Leader Board* in every department, to provide real-time ranking of everyone in the department based on the number of keystrokes recorded on their computers.
- No building access after 7:15AM.
- Encourage employees to pick out their next day's wardrobe at night so they don't waste time on it in the morning.
- Replace hallway carpets with ball-bearings for faster travel between departments.
- Program all phones to auto-disconnect after two minutes to keep conversations short and to-the-point.

- Reduce food offerings in the cafeterias to one item only. Serve all beverages in one, pre-dispensed size. Eliminates time wasted deciding what to order.
- Install business phones and computers in bathroom stalls.

"If we do it my way, we'll free up millions of dollars of employee time every year. Let's win one for the Gripper! Thank you."

When Grip finished, the audience erupted in laughter. Grip left the stage with a bewildered look, thinking he must have missed a joke someone told.

"Now, Rolly Burnrock will speak." Ted said as Rolly took the microphone.

"The NoMo Program? It's chicken shit compared to the $5 billion net income we produce each year. We're not doing it for the $10 million. We're doing it because of the attitude those things have created in you. This company was built on hard work, honesty, humility and creativity. The benefits I'm eliminating have dulled your drive. If you don't like the changes, Get Out! We're not going to implement any of the Gripper's productivity ideas. There's more wasted productivity by the 200 people in this room than by the other 40,000 employees of this company combined! I don't have the slightest idea what most of you do. How can we have this many people paid this kind of money and the CEO has not heard of a single distinguishing thing you have done this year? How is it that an individual like Richard Shunk can be a Senior Executive at this company and disappear for hours on end, but there is no impact to the work? Should I believe he is the only stealth executive here? Starting today, we're implementing a semi-annual value program: If you cannot quantify and justify the value you are adding, two times per year, then Get Out!

"Be very clear. These changes are not a reflection on the 40,000 employees who do the real work. The changes are a reflection of the entitlement society that has built up in this room. If I hear of any "shit rolls down hill" consequences to your employees, you will be told to Get Out!"

Rolly met with Ted and Tom when the meeting was over.

"You've let this company go soft. It is up to the two of you to implement and expand the direction I set this morning." Rolly said. "Ted, I want your recommendations on strategies to reduce the number of Senior Executives by 25%. Tom, you are to cut back on the aesthetics. I set the example by foregoing replacement of the Faberge Egg. I want your recommendations on strategies to generate $300 million in savings from infrastructure re-alignment. We have a great product and a great company, and you two need to start positioning us for long-term growth. Meeting over."

Chapter 30 – Clover & Jungle

The day after the SMMM, Rolly decided to walk to Grayson & Son to pick out some new suits. He was about to leave his office when Helen burst in, more excited than he had ever seen her.

"Rolly! The White House is on the phone for you! It might be the President!"

"Thank you, Helen. Have a seat before you start to hyperventilate." Rolly said before picking up the call.

"This is Rolly Burnrock."

"Please hold for Mr. Cladfaddle," an Operator said.

"Rolly? Hawkins Cladfaddle, Deputy Chief Of Staff for the President! Call me Hawk. The President asked me to call you to express his thanks for participatin' in the Summer Economic Summit and for your support in his landslide re-election. He's puttin' together his team for the second term and wants you as his Ambassador to the Republic Of Ireland. The President wanted to phone you himself, but his schedule is crazier than a barn full of wild dogs and cats. He asked me to extend this offer to you and told me to report back to him immediately with your answer or he was gonna string me AND you up by our privates in one of them big trees out there on the South Lawn. So what's it gonna be, Hoss? You puttin' a dog in this hunt or you gonna stay on the sidelines and drool on yourself?"

"Please extend my congratulations to the President on his re-election. I would be honored to be his Ambassador. What happens next?"

"You'll receive one of them Notices of Appointment by messenger and will be invited to the State Department for a briefing about what an Ambassador does. After the inauguration, you'll be invited to the White House to be officially credentialed by the President. In addition to the embassy staff, you'll get an assistant to handle all your personal arrangements, or as we call it, the shovel work. I suggest you get started on that right away. On behalf of the President, thank you for being of service to your country. I've got to go. The truck dealer called and my new pick-up is ready."

At the same time Rolly was on the phone with the Hawk, Barney O'Farkle was having a staff meeting in the Morale Enhancement department.

"Amma the last item on me meetin list is about a meetin I was in yesterday. I was in a meetin with Mr. Burnrock, ya know! He told me there's gonna be some belt-tightenin around here. We're gonna circle the wagons and put a ringed fence around it and lash right into things, ya know! We're gonna pull our long-johns up and put some starch in our stockings. We're gonna button up our coats and ammmmmm straighten our collars. We're gonna polish our spurs and saddles. He said it's absolutely phenomenally of the highest amma amma priority to dive into these things and get them done and dusted. He said a lot of you aren't goin at the same speed as you used to go and he wants you to put more horse power into the things you're doin and some such. He said that some employees would be showed the amma amma amma door if they're not lashin into things, ya know! He was happier than a leprechaun covered in candy clovers with all the senior executives like me-self, ya know and wants the amma amma employee staff clerk types like you to push ahead with all full steam. He said that it's gonna be"

"Excuse me, Mr. O'Farkle. Mr. Burnrock is on your line and said it was urgent." Barney's secretary interrupted.

"**What?** Where is it where my phone is?" Barney said, standing up so fast that his huge gut, which was lodged under the conference table, lifted the table off the floor and spilled everyone's papers on the floor.

"Amma amma amma this is Bar"

"Barney! Cut the blabbering. I just got off the phone with the President. He's naming me Ambassador to Ireland. You're going to be my assistant. I need you to get over there right away and get the lay of the land. You'll be with First Galaxy for two more weeks and after that, you're an employee of the State Department."

"Amma amma that's absolutely phenomenal, Rolly, I mean ammmm, Mr. Burnrock. How did Ted Reilly know your goin to the mother country?"

"The President of the United States, you moron, not the president of First Galaxy! If you have any more questions, call one of my assistants. I want you over there tomorrow." Rolly said as he hung up. *That's one way of getting some of the dead wood out of here,* Rolly thought. *Now I'm stuck with him, but I can keep him busy peeling potatoes.*

The next day, Barney was en route to Ireland. Late in the afternoon, Rolly received another phone call from The White House.

"Mr. Burnrock, this is the White House Operator. Please hold for the President."

"Burny, how are you? I want to thank you for your support during the campaign. My staff and I were reviewing the list of Ambassador Appointments and I had a damn good idea. With all the good work you do in the community, it would be a waste of your talents to go to a developed country. We need you in an area of the world that is still developing. That is why I am releasing a statement today announcing that you will be the new Ambassador to Zimbabwe. Look, I've got the Russian President holding on the other line. We'll get together after the inauguration. Congratulations and welcome to the Federal Government!" The President said and hung up.

"Rolly, was that The President?" Helen asked excitedly.

"Yes, Helen."

"What did he say?"

"Get a message to Barney O'Farkle. Tell him to head to Harare, Zimbabwe."

THE END

About the Author

Chuck Noranel has over 20 years experience in banking, financial services and education. He has received numerous awards for business and customer service contributions and accomplishments.

Blessed with the gift of keen observation and a twisted sense of humor, he is able to provide a unique insider's view into the highest levels of business.

Chuck lives with his family in Newark, Delaware.

Printed in the United States
33986LVS00003B/112

9 781420 828566